Eat Cheap but Eat Well

Charles Mattocks with Mary Hunt

EAT CHEAP but
EAT WELL

Charles Mattocks with Mary Hunt

WILEY

JOHN WILEY & SONS, INC.

Copyright © 2009 by Charles Mattocks. All rights reserved.

Published by John Wiley & Sons, Inc., Hoboken, New Jersey
Published simultaneously in Canada

For general information on our other products and services or for technical support, please contact our Customer Care Department within the United States at (800) 762-2974, outside the United States at (317) 572-3993 or fax (317) 572-4002.

Wiley also publishes its books in a variety of electronic formats. Some content that appears in print may not be available in electronic books. For more information about Wiley products, visit our web site at www.wiley.com.

Library of Congress Cataloging-in-Publication Data
Mattocks, Charles.
   Eat cheap but eat well / Charles Mattocks with Mary Hunt.
     p. cm.
   Includes index.
   ISBN 978-0-470-29336-2 (pbk. : alk. paper)
1. Low budget cookery. 2. Poor chef (Television program) 3. Cookery, International.
   I. Hunt, Mary, 1948- II. Title.
   TX652.M29746 2009
   641.5'52--dc22

2008012189

Printed in the United States of America
10 9 8 7 6 5 4 3 2 1

Of course I dedicate this to the two women who truly touch my world every day: my beautiful wife, Jasmina, who has changed my life and made me a better person, and our beautiful baby girl, Issabella. — CM

In memory of my dad, who taught me to try everything; and for my two favorite picky eaters, Mom and Jessica. —MH

Charles Mattocks and his wife, Jasmina

I would like to thank some amazing people who helped me & **Eat Cheap but Eat Well** become a project that has helped change my life and the lives of the ones I love,

as well as the many people from around the country who have supported the show and me in my dreams and endeavors.

It all started with my son, Armani. I moved to Florida and he helped me to become a good father and to come up with this amazing concept. I also want to thank Karen Saddow for the long hours and days of putting her heart and soul into something that we knew would be a hit. She believed in me and put up with the good and the hard times it took to get here. Thanks to Faye Bender, my literary agent, for helping this book get made, and I also have to say a big thanks to Mary Hunt, who took my words and recipes and made sense of it all.

I want to thank Justin Schwartz from Wiley for taking a chance on me and this dream of mine; I won't let you guys down. Thanks to Paige, for the long hours of work and meetings and having to listen to me rant all the time; Scott from Jah Beanz; and the guys at Everglades for The Poor Chef seasoning, especially Lanette and Michelle Cooper.

A TV show called *Daytime* in Tampa gave me my break with a great segment that helped launch me to the level I am at now, so to Lindsey, April, Steve D., and Marci, the producer, I say thanks for seeing something special in me.

To my mom, I have to say that I truly love you. You have been my greatest support without saying a word. Thanks also to my li'l baby sister who's not so little anymore, Shay Shay, and my dad.

Thanks also must go to the many producers, lawyers, and agents who kept my spirits up and showed support for the project, including Daniel Paul and E Love, and LL Cool J for expanding my mind to help me be the best I can be.

And also to all these folks: Stephanie Odom; Dan "the man" Crall for just being a great person and friend; Brother T, Monika, and the kids for being a family to me; Chuck in Tampa; David Ramos and his wife; Curtis Brown and Dave Constable; Belem; Gina; Lauren Fix; Dr. Bart Raddamaker; Jackie from Aging Backwards; Sharon Coleman; Marilee K.; Terri Williams; director Bill Duke for expanding my vision of how big this concept could truly be; boxing champ Antonio Tarver for coming on my show; Ian Beckels; James Woods and Arthur Sidelman; my family in Germany, daddy Arif and Demila; my brothers and sisters in Knollwood and Crenshaw Lake; Nate and Rachel Johnson; Kelly Hall for just being a great and wonderful friend and support; my brother Delany Yearger; Howard "the water doc" Fagre; Richard Mertz and his mom for running around town with me, getting it done; my big brother Andrew, I love you; James "big-up" Tomlin, my buddy, for being there and helping in every way—you never let me down and have been the show's biggest fan.

Also Jamal Forte; Eric Hall; Earl Christie of the Jets; Cousin Danny in South Carolina and Cousin Tracy in Canada; Angela Thomas for helping me get into this entertainment business—all these people in some way helped me with this book and with the evolution of *The Poor Chef* by being there for me or by contributing time and effort to the show.

Special thanks go to my family, the Marleys, and my uncle, the great Bob Marley—it was he who inspired me to want to touch the world. We met just twice, but he changed my life. He made me realize I had something special to do, and that with the help of God and hard work I could one day do something that would leave a mark on this planet—perhaps only a watermark, but nonetheless an impact that could lead the next generation of dreamers to see that it can be done. He once wrote to me and said, "To my nephew whom I love and support, Jah guide and protect." Uncle, those words changed my life; I hope to see you in paradise.

— Charles Mattocks

CELEBRATING
the Poor Chef
IN ALL OF US

My journey into what has come to be known as "**The Poor Chef**" started when I became a single dad. I'd been in the entertainment industry, living in Los Angeles,

with all the trappings of that lifestyle, but now there was something more important I needed to do. I knew deep down I wanted to raise my boy in a more normal and nurturing environment, so I decided to start over in Florida, near my mother and older brother.

I'd never been much of a cook, despite all the great cooks in my family—my grandmother in particular. I'm not sure whether it was their culture or my own lack of interest that kept me from being taught their kitchen secrets, but now I had a boy to raise. Unless I wanted to turn us into the king and prince of take-out, I needed to get comfortable in the kitchen, and I figured it wouldn't hurt if he did, too.

When I was on my own, I did the bachelor thing: I ate out, ordered in, or bought TV dinners. My idea of kitchen creativity was adding hot sauce to something fresh from the microwave in order to give it some personality. Not only would feeding two that way be a challenge to my starting-over budget, but I also knew it wouldn't be healthy for a child. (When I stopped to think about it, I knew it wasn't very healthy for me, either.) So I decided to cook for my son.

Fortunately, the first thing I tried was a success, at least from his perspective. That, more than anything, is probably what kept me going. That first meal was my grandmother's chicken curry. Hers was fantastic. I didn't think my version tasted much like it, but my son thought it was good and often asked me to make it. After a while I would just glumly stare at the pan—having had the real thing, I knew that my version was relatively bland. Unfortunately, I was pretty clueless about what to do about it.

So I got hooked on watching the cooking shows on TV. I didn't try to make their recipes, but I was fascinated with the idea of being creative in the kitchen and with the smatterings of culinary history. I liked the idea that behind all the new innovations, there are culinary traditions that go back to our simplest roots—that spices were used to tempt the palates of the pharaohs of Egypt, and that many types of cooking were developed in order to make inexpensive foods taste better. Further, I realized that a lot of so-called modern and convenience foods have less nutrition than the foods eaten by previous generations.

I was a lot less interested in the complexity, sophistication, and cost of most of the dishes I saw being prepared on TV. There's a disconnect between the people who watch and the people who cook. Many of these programs appeal to "armchair cooks" in the same way that glossy magazines appeal to "armchair travelers"—they represent the fascination people have with things they will probably never themselves experience. It's not real life; it's escape.

Because I'd had quite a bit of experience in front of the camera, I started thinking about what kind of cooking show could capture real life and still be fun. My son gave me the idea when we went into one of those restaurants with an open kitchen, all the white-hatted chefs hard at work performing feats of culinary art. My son said, "Wouldn't it be cool to watch real people cooking?" And I thought, yes, that would be very cool. Certainly, it would be more like the way most people learn to cook—by observing the good cooks in their families, by asking for a friend's recipe, by trial and error.

Another disconnect I've noticed is that cooking shows are more popular than ever, but people seem to be cooking less than ever. So many young people, in particular, live take-out or microwave lives. Meanwhile, obesity and its related health problems such as diabetes are at an all-time high, becoming an American epidemic.

From the beginnings of recorded time, meals have been central to human culture. Kings and their soldiers sat down to a feast before going into battle. Meals fortified the family for going into the fields to raise their crops or tend their animals. We give food in sympathy to those in mourning. For celebration, we make a special meal or bake a cake. I wanted there to be a cooking show that would celebrate regular people and the recipes handed down in their families, their versions of familiar favorites, and the ethnic variations to which many of us have still not been exposed. I wanted to use food as a way to bridge the gap between cultures, to allow all sorts of people from all sorts of backgrounds and with all sorts of income levels to share their kitchen secrets. I wanted to watch and learn from all those people—and I wanted to celebrate them.

I started to talk with everyone I knew about what they cooked, and I learned some interesting things. One was that, when I talked about recipes for television, they immediately thought I wanted their fanciest and most elaborate recipes. The other was that, once they realized I wanted to learn about "real food," the cost of those recipes was considerably less.

I also learned, from history and from other cultures, that it's the American obsession with meat that adds most of the dollars—and a lot of the calories and fat—to our culinary budgets. If you say to an American, "Can you make dinner for four people for $7?" his or her immediate reaction is to think, "Gosh, no, the meat alone will cost that much." That's because most meats cost at least $2 a pound (usually more)—and because Ameri-

cans tend to allow a half-pound (8 ounces) of meat as a portion. In most parts of the world, and even according to the United States Department of Agriculture's own food pyramid, a serving of meat is considered to be about 3 ounces.

If I told people the meat would be free, I found, most thought they could manage to make a nice meal with $5 more. So I started presenting people with this challenge: "Imagine you're a poor chef. Come up with a meal for two or four people for under $7." People rose to that challenge, and so The Poor Chef was born.

Many of today's traditional and favorite recipes have their roots in economic necessity. Stews and pot roasts were developed as ways to tenderize tougher (and cheaper) cuts of meat. Slow roasting brought out the flavor of the meat of older animals—our ancestors didn't have the luxury of butchering an animal until it was full grown and had brought forth a new generation. Fajitas were developed by Mexican cowboys who were given only the toughest parts of the cow to eat. It was scavengers who, of necessity, first found foods today considered delicacies—who but a starving person would think, let me try that oyster? That seaweed?

RECIPE COSTS >

¢ under **$5** for **4** servings

$ under **$7** for **4** servings

$$ under **$7** for **2** servings

Sauces and spices were developed as camouflage. Smoking and salting were methods of preserving foods developed before the existence of refrigeration. Economy breeds creativity.

They say that rich people stay that way because they know when to spend money—and when not to spend it. The converse is also true: Many people feel poorer than they really are because they spend unnecessarily. Take the "Poor Chef challenge" and rediscover the fact that most meals don't have to cost a lot of money. An expression I like to use is, "Eat cheap, but eat well." The recipes in this cookbook can all be made for no more than $3.50 per person, and in most cases much less. (I also show how you can splurge, or where you can cut costs further.)

One of the most common reasons why Americans overspend is that we can find almost any food, at any time, in our markets. We've gotten into the habit of eating food out of season, and that taxes our budgets unnecessarily. Fresh fruits and vegetables are much more affordable when they aren't being imported across long distances. How do you break the habit? Don't go to the store with a specific menu in mind, paying whatever they ask. Shop the specials and the seasonal produce and think about what you can prepare with them that's within your repertoire.

That's what *Eat Cheap but Eat Well* is—a way to broaden your repertoire. It's not all about having an infinite number of recipes. It's about sharing ideas, cooking with love, and economizing without sacrificing nutrition.

The recipes in this book bridge the gap between cultures, celebrate the creativity of real people I've met, and, I hope, will entice people back into the kitchen rather than intimidating them, at the same time putting smiles on our children's faces while nourishing their bodies.

Another of my Poor Chef slogans is "from trailer park to Beverly Hills in search of America's best budget meals." People from all walks of life have shared their recipes with me. I continue to visit their homes all across the country—and, I hope someday, around the world—to learn from them, and to share what I learn with all of you.

POULTRY
with
PIZZAZZ

"We could probably cook chicken every day of the year without repeating ourselves."

Chicken is probably the most versatile meat in any home chef's repertoire. It's tasty enough to stand on its own but readily adapts to a variety of accompanying

flavors—it's sort of a character actor rather than a big-name movie star.

Poultry, especially chicken, is found in the cuisine of almost every ethnicity, and that's why there's such a diversity of recipes. In fact, the choice is overwhelming—we could probably cook chicken every day of the year without repeating ourselves. Of course, our families probably wouldn't be very happy about an all-chicken-all-the-time approach.

While the poultry category includes a lot of different birds, from squab to turkey, chicken is the most readily available and usually the least expensive. It's often cheapest to buy it bone-in, but do the math: Figure that 70 percent of the weight of a boneless chicken breast is meat, while only about 50 percent of the weight of a whole chicken is meat. In other words, if you can find boneless chicken that costs less than 50 percent more by the pound than the bone-in variety, it's a bargain and you should grab it.

Another way to get more bang for your buck is to cook a whole chicken in a stockpot with water and vegetables. When the chicken is cooked, you can save the meat to use in salads, pasta dishes, etc., and you can save the broth—freeze it in small plastic containers, making sure to leave room for expansion—to use in recipes.

When cooking poultry any way other than as a simple roasted bird, first remove the skin and fat. With so many seasonings, sauces, and salsas that you can add to poultry, you don't need the skin for flavor, and the fat and calories are just unnecessary. You can eat quite a bit more skinless chicken than you can other meats for the same amount of calories, which makes it a good option when someone is really hungry.

Turkey isn't just for holidays, either. You can adapt just about any chicken recipe to turkey, and the larger pieces give you a few extra visual options for slicing turkey into "steaks" or kebab cubes; be creative. If you find a good buy on a whole turkey, don't be intimidated by its size; ask the butcher (most supermarkets will do this for you) to cut it in half or in pieces for easier freezing.

TIPS >
Don't forget to wash anything raw chicken comes in contact with (including your hands). This is extremely important in preventing cross-contamination and food-borne illnesses.

CARIBBEAN LIME CHICKEN WITH GRILLED PINEAPPLE

This dish is colorful, with sweet and savory elements, and is really easy to make. We like to make it with pimientos—the smaller, sweeter cousin of bell peppers—which you can even buy already diced in a jar, but using a fresh red bell pepper is usually more economical. You can also cut the remaining bell pepper into rings or strips to decorate the dish or save it for another use. Kiwi gives the recipe some extra tropical flavor and looks pretty, but it isn't an essential ingredient; if you want to use something with a similar texture, you can try sliced strawberries, or omit it altogether.

4 SERVINGS **$**

- 4 boneless, skinless chicken breast halves (about 1 pound total)
- ½ cup lime juice (about 4 limes)
- ½ red bell pepper, seeded and diced (or one 4-ounce jar diced red pimientos, drained)
- 1 teaspoon minced garlic
- 1 teaspoon freshly ground black pepper
- 1 10-ounce can sliced pineapple in juice, juice reserved
- 2 kiwi fruits, peeled and sliced (optional)
- 1 tablespoon honey
- 1 to 2 cups hot cooked white rice

1. Place each chicken breast between two slices of waxed paper and flatten with a mallet or the bottom of a heavy pot to about half its original thickness. Arrange all the chicken in a lightly greased 9 x 13-inch baking dish. In a small bowl, mix together the lime juice, bell pepper, garlic, black pepper, and juice from the pineapple. Pour over the chicken. Cover and marinate in the refrigerator for at least 4 hours or overnight, turning once.

2. Preheat the broiler and set the rack so that the top of your pan will be 6 inches from the heat source.

3. If necessary, spoon off and discard enough of the marinade so that the tops of the chicken pieces are exposed. Arrange the pineapple and kiwi slices, if using, on top of the chicken. In a small bowl, mix together the honey with 1 tablespoon water and microwave for 10 to 15 seconds, until the honey is dissolved in the water. Pour the honey glaze evenly over the chicken and fruit.

4. Broil for 15 to 20 minutes, or until the chicken is cooked through, basting occasionally to prevent burning. If the top browns too rapidly, move the pan to a lower rack.

5. Divide the rice among four plates. Cut each chicken breast in half and serve the chicken on top of the rice. Spoon additional pan drippings over the top as desired.

WEST INDIAN CHICKEN CURRY FLURRY

4 SERVINGS **$**

Curry and coconut are a winning combination. While genuine coconut milk is always preferable, for cooking you can make a substitute for coconut milk out of ingredients that you may already have on hand. If you are using cow's milk or soy milk, for each ½ cup add 1 teaspoon coconut extract and a dash of sugar or other sweetener (if you're using skim milk, stir in ⅛ teaspoon cornstarch or arrowroot, too). For a visual change of pace, you can cut the chicken into strips instead of cubes. You can also make this recipe with leftover cooked chicken, in which case you'll need to simmer it for only about 5 minutes in the second step. For vegetarians, this recipe is also great when made with one pound of cubed firm tofu instead of the chicken.

3   or 4 boneless, skinless chicken breast halves (¾ to 1 pound total), cut into 2-inch cubes

1   medium onion, chopped (about ½ cup)

4   teaspoons minced garlic

1   tablespoon grated fresh ginger

1   tablespoon Creole seasoning

2   tablespoons canola oil

2   tablespoons curry powder

1   cup coconut milk

1   tablespoon light brown sugar

1   chicken bouillon cube

2   cups hot cooked white rice

1. Place the chicken pieces into a medium-size mixing bowl. Add the onion, 3 teaspoons of the minced garlic, the ginger, and Creole seasoning. Mix well and set aside.

2. Heat the oil in a large skillet over medium heat until it shimmers. Add the remaining 1 teaspoon garlic and cook, stirring, until it turns golden brown, 2 to 3 minutes. Add the curry powder, chicken mixture, and ⅔ cup water. Simmer, covered, for 15 to 20 minutes, or until the chicken is cooked through, adding additional water a little bit at a time as necessary if the ingredients start to stick to the pan.

3. Add the coconut milk, brown sugar, and bouillon cube and stir well. Simmer, uncovered, until the bouillon cube has dissolved and the sauce has thickened, about 10 minutes longer.

4. Spoon the chicken mixture over the rice to serve.

TIPS >
If you don't like actually eating garlic and prefer to just use it for flavor, cut a clove of garlic into large slices for cooking and then you can remove them from a sauce before serving.

DAYS-GONE-BY CHICKEN AND DUMPLINGS

This hearty stew substitutes dumplings for the potatoes commonly used in beef stews. To make sure dumplings come out right, two things are important. First, don't overmix the dough or your dumplings will be tough. Second, at the end of the suggested cooking time, remove one dumpling and cut it in half to make sure it's no longer doughy. If it is, cook the rest for another minute or two. The double-strength chicken broth is important for giving the dumplings enough flavor; make it by either boiling down a gallon of regular-strength chicken broth to half the volume, or by adding one chicken bouillon cube for each cup of broth.

4 SERVINGS $

1 2- to 3-pound frying
   chicken, whole or in pieces
8 cups (2 quarts) double-
   strength chicken broth
   (see headnote)
3 cups chopped celery
3 cups chopped onions
1 cup peeled sliced carrots
1½ teaspoons poultry
   seasoning
1 teaspoon celery seed
¾ teaspoon freshly ground
   black pepper
   Salt

For Dumplings:
1½ cups all-purpose flour
1 tablespoon baking powder
½ teaspoon salt
¼ cup vegetable shortening
½ to ⅔ cup ice water
1 cup half-and-half
½ cup all-purpose flour
2 tablespoons minced fresh
   parsley

1. Wash the chicken and remove the giblets. If necessary, cut the chicken into pieces at every joint. Put the chicken pieces and giblets into a large stockpot. Add the broth and 2 cups each of the celery and onions. Bring to a boil, cover, reduce the heat to medium-low, and simmer for 45 minutes.

2. Remove the chicken to a large bowl or plate and set aside to cool. When the chicken has cooled down, remove and discard the skin and bones, and cut the chicken meat into bite-size pieces. Cover and set aside. Strain the broth, saving only the liquid.

3. Measure 6 cups of the reserved broth into a clean stockpot. (Freeze any remaining broth for use at a later date.) Add the rest of the celery and onions, the carrots, poultry seasoning, celery seed, and pepper; add salt to taste. Bring to a full boil. Cover; reduce the heat and simmer until the vegetables are barely tender, about 20 minutes.

4. While the vegetables are cooking, prepare the dumplings. Combine 1½ cups of the flour, baking soda, and salt in a medium-size mixing bowl. Cut in the shortening bit by bit with a fork or pastry blender until the mixture is crumbly. Using a fork, mix in just enough of the ice water to make a soft, biscuit-like dough.

5. In a mixing bowl, whisk together the half-and-half and the remaining ½ cup flour, and add to the stock. Bring the stock to a boil and simmer, stirring frequently, until thickened, 3 to 5 minutes. Add the chicken. Drop the dumpling dough by rounded tablespoonfuls onto the gently bubbling stew, spacing them out so they don't stick together. Cover and simmer over medium-low heat for 15 minutes (do not release steam by lifting the lid).

6. Serve in bowls with the dumplings evenly distributed. Sprinkle with the parsley.

And here's a tip for adding flour as a thickener: It gets lumpy when it's at a different temperature than the liquid it's to thicken. In step 5 here, you have two options. You can either warm the half-and-half in the top of a double boiler before stirring in the flour (if you use the microwave, be careful not to cook the cream), or you can gradually stir several teaspoons of the broth, 1 teaspoon at a time, into the cream-flour mixture to raise its temperature and then gradually stir the whole thing back into the stockpot.

MUST-HAVE-SECONDS CHICKEN WAIKIKI

4 SERVINGS   **$**

Cultures around the world have their own twists on similar ingredients. This recipe has the same core components as West Indian chicken curry—chicken, pineapple, brown sugar—but ingredients from the Pacific Rim give this a Polynesian flair. In Hawaii they use macadamia nuts for this recipe, but cashews or peanuts are equally good—use whichever is handy and fits your budget. If you prefer to cook without alcohol, for 1 cup of sherry you can substitute a mixture of ½ cup vinegar, ½ cup water, and 2 tablespoons sugar. You can also make this with bone-in chicken breasts, in which case you'll need 1 to 1¼ pounds. Jasmine rice is a long-grain rice with a slightly nutty flavor, less sticky than white rice; you can substitute basmati rice, brown rice, or any long-grain rice.

- 4 boneless, skinless chicken breast halves (¾ to 1 pound total)
- 1 cup dry sherry
- 1 teaspoon crushed dried rosemary
- ¼ teaspoon salt
- ⅛ teaspoon freshly ground black pepper
- 1 cup orange juice
- 1 tablespoon lime juice
- 1 tablespoon light soy sauce
- ⅓ cup firmly packed dark brown sugar
- 1 tablespoon cornstarch
- 1 10-ounce can pineapple chunks, drained
- 2 kiwi fruits, peeled and cut into chunks (optional)
- 2 cups hot cooked jasmine rice (or other long-grain rice)
- ¼ cup macadamia nuts, cashews, or peanuts, coarsely chopped

1. Preheat the oven to 350° F.

2. Place the chicken breasts in a lightly greased 9 x 13-inch baking dish. Pour the sherry over the chicken. Sprinkle with the rosemary, salt, and pepper. Cover with aluminum foil and bake for 25 minutes, occasionally basting with the sherry.

3. While the chicken is baking, mix together the orange juice, lime juice, and soy sauce in a small saucepan. In a separate bowl, mix together the brown sugar with the cornstarch until there are no lumps, then stir into the orange juice mixture. Cook over medium heat until thickened, stirring constantly to avoid any lumps. Remove from the heat and stir in the pineapple and kiwi, if using.

4. Remove and discard the foil cover from the chicken. Pour the sauce mixture over the chicken and bake for another 15 to 20 minutes, until the chicken is cooked through.

5. Serve over the rice and garnish with the nuts.

PAPAYA-MANGO CHICKEN

You can use a whole cut-up fryer for this recipe, or whatever chicken pieces you want (for example, you can often find packages of thighs or drumsticks on sale). Cut the chicken pieces into their smallest components (i.e., separate wings from breasts, or cut legs into two pieces at the joint). Rice absorbs some of the sauce nicely, but there's no reason you couldn't serve this over egg noodles or pasta instead.

4 SERVINGS **$**

1 tablespoon canola oil
2 pounds chicken pieces
1 cup orange juice
½ cup light brown sugar
⅓ cup lemon juice (3 to 4 lemons)
1 tablespoon cornstarch
1 mango, peeled, seeded, and chopped
1 small papaya, peeled, seeded, and chopped
2 cups hot cooked rice or pasta
Fresh mint leaves for garnish

1. Preheat the oven to 350°F.
2. Heat the oil in a large skillet over medium-high heat. Add the chicken pieces and cook, turning to brown on all sides. Transfer the chicken to a lightly greased 9 x 13-inch baking dish. Bake for 30 minutes.
3. While the chicken is baking, combine the orange juice, brown sugar, lemon juice, and cornstarch in a saucepan. Bring to a boil over medium heat, stirring constantly. Stir in the mango and papaya and pour over the chicken. Bake for 10 more minutes.
4. Serve the chicken over the rice or pasta, spooning the fruit sauce over all. Garnish with mint leaves.

Chicken is probably the most versatile meat in any home chef's repertoire.

CRUNCHY CASHEW CHICKEN WITH FRUIT SALSA

Nut crunch, fruit, and coconut are an unbeatable combination. You can prepare the chicken breasts ahead of time and refrigerate them, covered, for as long as overnight; chilling them helps the coating set, though it's not required. If corn-flakes aren't handy, you can use almost any other kind of crispy cereal flakes. You can also substitute peanuts for the cashews. The salsa can be made up to a day ahead. And if the fruit for the salsa is out of season and expensive, in a pinch you can use just chopped oranges with the mint and lemon juice.

4 $ SERVINGS

1⅓ cup cornflakes
⅓ cup cashews
1 teaspoon ground ginger
⅛ teaspoon salt
 Freshly ground black pepper
1 large egg plus 1 egg white
4 boneless, skinless chicken breast halves (about 1 pound total)

For Coconut Rice:
1 cup white rice (not instant)
2 cups coconut milk

For Fruit Salsa:
1 cup sliced fresh strawberries
2 kiwi fruits, peeled and diced
1 banana, peeled and sliced
2 or 3 fresh mint leaves, crushed
2 tablespoons lemon juice

1. Preheat the oven to 375°F.

2. Process the cornflakes and cashews together in a food processor or blender until they are reduced to fine crumbs. Add the ginger, salt, and a pinch of pepper to the cashew mix and pulse briefly to blend. Dump onto a shallow plate.

3. In a small bowl, combine the egg and egg white with a splash of water. Brush each chicken breast half with the egg, then roll in the nut mixture to coat. Place the coated chicken in a lightly greased 9 x13-inch baking dish and bake for about 30 minutes, or until cooked through.

4. While the chicken is baking, cook the rice according to the package directions, substituting coconut milk for the water called for in the directions.

5. While the rice is cooking, mix the fruit salsa ingredients together in a medium-size bowl.

6. Serve the chicken over the rice and spoon the fruit salsa over the top.

COUNTRY COQ AU VIN

Coq au vin—French for "chicken with wine"—is actually French country home cooking. Basically, it's chicken stew. As with many international dishes, however, what's simple home cooking in one place can be a special and unusual—but still economical—dish when it's far from home. Also, keep in mind that they're not cooking with expensive wines in those French country farmhouses; they're cooking with whatever is inexpensive and readily available, so you should do the same.

An easy way to peel lots of little onions is to place them in a colander and pour boiling water over them. Once you trim the ends, the papery coating should peel off easily.

4 SERVINGS · $

2   teaspoons salt
¼   teaspoon ground cloves or allspice
¼   teaspoon freshly ground black pepper
1   2- to 3-pound frying chicken, whole or in pieces
    Tarragon vinegar
3   tablespoons butter or olive oil
12 small white onions
1   clove garlic, chopped
1½ cups dry red wine
8   to 12 whole baby carrots
1   stalk celery including leaves, sliced
1   tablespoon sugar
1   tablespoon dried marjoram
1   tablespoon minced fresh parsley or 1 teaspoon dried parsley
½   bay leaf
    Pinch of dried thyme
24 button mushrooms
8   ounces wide egg noodles

1. In a small bowl, combine the salt, cloves, and pepper. Wash the chicken and remove the giblets. If necessary, cut the chicken into pieces at every joint. Rub the spice mixture into the chicken pieces. Sprinkle the chicken with tarragon vinegar.

2. In a large skillet, melt the butter or heat the oil over medium heat. Add the onions and garlic and cook, stirring, until the onions are lightly browned. With a slotted spoon, transfer the onions to a Dutch oven or heatproof covered 4-quart casserole dish.

3. Using tongs, add the chicken pieces a few at a time to the fat in the skillet, transferring them to the Dutch oven when browned on both sides. Continue until all the chicken pieces have been browned.

4. Pour the wine over the chicken. Set over medium heat. Add the carrots and celery to the pot. Stir in the sugar, marjoram, parsley, bay leaf, and thyme. When the liquid begins to simmer, cover the pot, adjust the heat if necessary, and continue to simmer, covered, until the chicken begins to fall off the bone, 45 minutes to 1 hour. Add the mushrooms about 10 minutes before the chicken is done.

5. While the chicken is cooking, boil water for the egg noodles and prepare according to the package directions. Drain and toss with a little oil to keep from sticking together; put in a large shallow bowl or platter. Cover with aluminum foil to keep warm.

6. Remove the chicken and the vegetables with a slotted spoon and set over the noodles; replace the foil cover. Strain the sauce to remove bones and spices and return the strained liquid to the pot over high heat. Boil until the sauce reduces by about one-half. Pour the sauce over the chicken and noodles and serve.

"I liked the idea that behind all the new innovations, there are culinary traditions that go back to our simplest roots."

GINGER CHICKEN WITH AVOCADO

Ginger, cumin, and coriander give this recipe an Indian flavor, so we like serving it with fragrant basmati rice. The avocado gives it a bit more color and flavor but can easily be omitted if it pushes your budget too far. This recipe can also be made with turkey: Cut 1 pound turkey breast into 4 equal pieces and proceed as for chicken.

4 ¢
SERVINGS

1 **tablespoon grated fresh ginger**
1 **teaspoon ground cumin**
4 **boneless, skinless chicken breast halves (about 1 pound total)**
1 **tablespoon olive oil**
1 **10.5-ounce can chicken broth**
1 **avocado, peeled and diced (optional)**
¼ **cup nonfat plain yogurt**
1 **tablespoon chopped fresh cilantro**
2 **teaspoons lime juice**
1 **teaspoon minced garlic**
2 **cups hot cooked basmati rice**

1. In a small bowl, mix together the ginger and cumin. Rub the chicken well on both sides with the mixture. **2.** Heat the oil in a large skillet over medium heat until it shimmers. Add the chicken and cook until browned, 2 to 3 minutes per side. Add the chicken broth to the skillet, cover, and simmer until the chicken is cooked through, 10 to 15 minutes. **3.** Meanwhile, in the small bowl of an electric mixer or in a blender, add the avocado, if using, the yogurt, cilantro, lime juice, and garlic and blend until smooth. **4.** Serve the chicken on a bed of the rice and spoon the avocado sauce over the top.

TIPS >
Don't go out and buy a specialty ingredient just for one recipe—that's a budget-buster. Wait until you know you have several recipes that call for it, and then buy it when you find a bargain.

PAPRIKA CHICKEN WITH SPAETZLE

This is an international recipe that's a variation on the classic Hungarian dish chicken paprikash. Paprika, a powder made from dried red peppers, is found in different variations in many countries. In North America the most commonly available paprika comes from Spain and Hungary. Real Hungarian paprika tends to be richer and sweeter than other varieties. Usually, the redder the paprika, the milder it is, while the light brown variants are the hottest.

Spaetzle is a nice accompaniment to this dish, but you can substitute cooked egg noodles. There's a special tool called a spaetzle press that makes the dough into strands, but you can easily approximate it with a large-holed colander. If it sounds like too much trouble and you don't mind spending a bit extra, you can also find ready-to-cook spaetzle in some stores.

4 SERVINGS $

1	2- to 3-pound frying chicken, whole or in pieces
2	tablespoons canola oil
1	large onion, chopped
¾	pound fresh tomatoes, seeded and chopped (or one 14-ounce can diced tomatoes, drained)
2	tablespoons paprika
1	teaspoon salt
¼	teaspoon freshly ground black pepper
1	chicken bouillon cube
1	green bell pepper, seeded and sliced
8	ounces low-fat sour cream

For Spaetzle:

2	cups all-purpose flour
4	large eggs, beaten
2	teaspoons salt
	Dash of freshly ground black pepper
1	tablespoon butter

1. Wash the chicken and remove the giblets. If necessary, cut the chicken into pieces at every joint. Heat the oil in a large skillet over medium-high heat. Add the chicken to the skillet and cook until lightly browned on all sides. Remove the chicken pieces to a large plate and set aside. Add the onion to the skillet and cook, stirring occasionally, until softened, about 2 minutes. Add ½ cup water, the tomatoes, paprika, salt, black pepper, and bouillon cube, and stir. Return the chicken to the skillet, stirring to coat. Heat until the liquid boils, then reduce the heat, cover, and simmer for about 20 minutes. Add the green pepper, cover, and simmer until the chicken is cooked through and the peppers are tender, 5 to 10 minutes. Stir in the sour cream and simmer for about 5 minutes.

2. While the chicken is cooking, prepare the spaetzle. Bring 4 quarts water to boil in a large pot. In a medium-size mixing bowl, add the flour, eggs, salt, and pepper with ½ cup water and stir to combine. Press the batter through a colander (see headnote), a few tablespoons at a time, into the boiling water, making strands. Boil, stirring occasionally, until the spaetzle rises to the surface and the pieces are no longer doughy, about 5 minutes. Drain and toss with the butter to prevent sticking.

3. Serve the chicken and the spaetzle together, spooning the sauce from the skillet over all.

LEMON-SAGE FILLET OF TURKEY

You can buy prepackaged turkey breast fillets, or you can cut ½-inch-thick slices from an uncooked turkey breast, which is usually more economical. To flatten fillets, if you don't have a meat mallet handy you can use the bottom of a heavy pot. To release the lemon juice easily, before cutting and squeezing, roll each lemon around on the counter while pressing it with the palm of your hand (if you squeeze by hand, using the back of a spoon inside the lemon halves will help release more juice).

This is a simple and subtle dish with elegant flavors. I like it served with noodles or pasta, but it would also go well with roasted baby potatoes.

4 SERVINGS ¢

1   **pound turkey breast fillets**
2   **teaspoons olive oil**
4   **lemons**
3   **tablespoons ground sage**
1   **teaspoon Dijon mustard**
½   **teaspoon salt**
¼   **teaspoon freshly ground
      black pepper**
6   **ounces dry egg noodles or
      pasta**
1   **pound green beans,
      trimmed**

1. Preheat the oven to 350°F.
2. Place the turkey fillets between two sheets of waxed paper and pound lightly with a mallet to no more than ½-inch thickness. Heat the oil in a large skillet over medium heat. Add the turkey fillets and cook until lightly browned, 2 to 3 minutes per side. Transfer the turkey to a lightly greased 9 x 13-inch baking dish.
3. In a small bowl, combine the juice of 3 of the lemons, the sage, mustard, salt, and pepper. Spread the lemon mixture over the browned turkey fillets. Cover the dish with aluminum foil and bake for about

30 minutes, or until the turkey is cooked through.
4. While the turkey is in the oven, prepare the noodles according to the package directions. Also, add the green beans to a steamer basket in a pot of simmering water; cover and steam until they are hot and just slightly tender. (Or you may stir-fry them briefly in 1 teaspoon oil in a skillet over medium-high heat until crisp-tender, about 3 minutes.)
5. Cut the remaining lemon into wedges. Serve the turkey with the noodles and green beans, and garnish with the lemon wedges.

LUTZ ORANGE GROVE CHICKEN

My friend Nathan Johnson, host of an up-and-coming TV show called *Camping People*, has an outdoorsy attitude that inspires his cooking. He created this recipe to use fruits that grow in his garden in Lutz, Florida. He says that if you aren't fortunate enough to be able to pick fruit from your own garden, your local fruit stand (in Florida and California, at the very least) will probably have fresher, cheaper oranges and limes than the supermarket. When choosing ripe plantains, look for ones with peels that are starting to turn brown.

2 **$**
SERVINGS

1   **whole boneless, skinless chicken breast (10 to 12 ounces), halved**
1   **cup fresh-squeezed orange juice**
3   **tablespoons butter**
    Salt and freshly ground white or black pepper
    Canola oil for frying
2   **ripe plantains, peeled and sliced at an angle**
½   **tablespoon all-purpose flour**
1   **teaspoon minced garlic**
1   **orange, seeded, peeled, and sliced, plus additional orange slices for garnish (optional)**
1   **tablespoon sugar**
1   **tablespoon soy sauce**
1   **tablespoon lime juice**
1   **cup hot cooked brown rice**

1. The day before you plan to serve, marinate the chicken in ½ cup of the orange juice in a covered bowl in the refrigerator overnight.

2. In a large skillet over medium-low heat, melt 2 tablespoons of the butter. Add the chicken and cook until browned, 2 to 3 minutes per side. Raise the heat to medium, cover, and continue cooking until the chicken's juices run clear when pricked and the meat is no longer pink inside, about 5 minutes. Sprinkle the chicken with two pinches of salt and a dash of pepper. Remove from the pan and let rest for about 10 minutes.

3. To the same skillet, add oil to a depth of about 1 inch. Heat the oil over medium-high heat until a drop of water makes it sputter. Add the plantain slices and cook until golden, 2 to 3 minutes per side. Drain the plantains on paper towels.

4. In a separate skillet, melt the remaining 1 tablespoon butter. Add the flour and garlic and cook, stirring, until browned. Add the remaining ½ cup orange juice along with the orange slices, sugar, soy sauce, and lime juice, stirring; simmer until smooth and thickened, about 3 minutes.

5. Cut the chicken into long strips. Serve over the rice and spoon the sauce over the chicken. Serve the fried plantains on the side. Garnish with orange slices, if desired.

CHICKEN KORMA AND VEGETABLE SABZI

This is my friend Nanda Kishore's version of a traditional Indian dish. "Every region in India has a distinct style and flavor and is largely influenced by locally available ingredients," says Kishore, who was born and raised in the south of India before moving to the United States in 1993.

While you can find garlic and ginger pastes in specialty stores or online, you can easily make a good substitute at home (make it all-in-one for greater convenience) if you have a coffee grinder or food processor. (A blender probably won't be up to the task of handling gingerroot.) Peel 4 cloves of garlic and visually estimate a similar amount of gingerroot. Peel and slice the ginger, then add the ginger and garlic to the grinder or processor and grind into a smooth paste.

4 SERVINGS $

¼ cup canola oil
1 large onion, chopped
1 teaspoon garlic paste (see headnote)
1 teaspoon ginger paste (see headnote)
1½ to 2 pounds bone-in chicken, cut into pieces at all joints
1 cup plain yogurt
1 teaspoon salt
1 teaspoon ground turmeric
1 teaspoon chili powder
1 teaspoon curry powder

For Vegetable Sabzi:
¼ cup canola oil
1 medium onion, chopped
1 teaspoon salt
1 teaspoon ground turmeric
1 teaspoon chili powder
1 medium head cauliflower, cored and separated into florets
1 cup shelled peas
2 cups hot cooked basmati rice

1. Heat the oil in a large skillet over medium heat. Add the onion and cook, stirring, until tender, about 5 minutes. Mix in the garlic paste and ginger paste, reduce the heat, and cook, stirring frequently, until the paste has melted into the oil.
2. Add the chicken, yogurt, salt, turmeric, chili powder, and curry powder and stir. Cover and cook over low heat until the chicken is cooked through, about 25 minutes.
3. While the chicken cooks, prepare the vegetable sabzi. Heat the oil in another large skillet over medium heat. Add the onion and cook, stirring, until tender, about 5 minutes. Add the salt, turmeric, and chili powder and stir until well blended. Stir in the cauliflower and peas. Cover and cook over low heat until the cauliflower is tender, about 20 minutes.
4. Serve the chicken with the vegetable sabzi and rice.

TURKEY-ZUCCHINI STIR-FRY

This dish is inspiring because it proves that you don't need a lot of vegetables to make a stir-fry work. You can also make it with leftover turkey (preferably the dark meat, which is more moist) or with chicken. If you don't have zucchini handy, try this with yellow summer squash or fresh green beans.

4 SERVINGS

2 **tablespoons cornstarch**
½ **cup chicken broth, at room temperature**
¼ **cup soy sauce**
2 **teaspoons sugar**
¼ **cup canola oil, plus more as needed**
2 **teaspoons grated fresh ginger**
2 **large zucchini, sliced into 2-inch-long strips**
1 **pound boneless, skinless turkey, cubed**
¼ **cup lemon juice**
2 **cups hot cooked brown rice**

1. Add the cornstarch to a small bowl and stir in ¼ cup of the chicken broth until the cornstarch dissolves. Add the soy sauce and sugar, stir, and set aside.

2. Add the oil to a wok or large slant-sided frying pan over medium-high heat. Once the oil sizzles, add the ginger and cook, stirring constantly, for 30 seconds. Add half of the zucchini strips and stir-fry until barely tender, about 3 minutes. With a slotted spoon or spatula, transfer the zucchini to a plate. Stir-fry the remaining zucchini strips, adding more oil if necessary, and transfer to the plate.

3. Add the turkey to the wok and stir-fry until cooked through, about 1 minute, adding oil as necessary. Add the soy sauce mixture and lemon juice, stirring constantly until the sauce thickens; if too thick, add the remaining broth. Return the zucchini to the wok, stir well to blend, reduce the heat to low, and cook for about 1 minute.

4. Serve the turkey and zucchini stir-fry over the rice.

LAUREN'S ENCHILADA CHICKEN

4 SERVINGS $

My friend Lauren Fix, journalist and TV's "The Car Coach," likes to create recipes, especially ones that kids will find yummy and, as she says, that painlessly sneak in some vegetables. I like this with whole wheat tortillas for the nutty taste they add, but any kind will do. It can be served by itself, or with rice and beans, or with a salad on the side.

We normally try to avoid using canned ingredients whenever possible, but it's always useful to have some recipes you can make last-minute from your pantry, such as this. If you have homemade tomato sauce handy, you can make your own enchilada sauce by heating 2 tablespoons of olive oil in a large frying pan, stirring in 2 tablespoons each of flour and chili powder until the flour is lightly browned, and then adding 1 cup each of tomato sauce and water, along with garlic powder and salt to taste; bring to a boil, then cover and simmer until the flavors are blended, about 10 minutes. To use fresh mushrooms, add ½ pound of sliced mushrooms when you add the chicken to the skillet.

2 tablespoons olive oil
1 pound boneless, skinless chicken breasts, diced
1 bunch scallions, sliced, dark green parts discarded
1 teaspoon ground cumin
1 teaspoon minced garlic
1 4.5-ounce can sliced mushrooms, drained
2 10-ounce cans enchilada sauce
8 ounces shredded Monterey Jack cheese (2 cups)
4 8-inch whole wheat tortillas
1 4.25-ounce can black olives, drained and sliced (optional)

1. Preheat the oven to 350°F.
2. Heat the oil in a large skillet over medium heat. Add the chicken, scallions, cumin, and garlic and cook, stirring, until the chicken is lightly browned on all sides. Stir in the mushrooms. Add 1 can of the enchilada sauce and half the cheese and reduce the heat to a simmer.
3. Meanwhile, pour a little of the enchilada sauce from the second can into the bottom of a lightly greased 9 x 13-inch baking dish.

4. Fill the tortillas with equal amounts of the chicken mixture. Roll each one up tightly and place, seam-side down, in the baking dish. Pour the remaining enchilada sauce over the top and bake for about 15 minutes, until the tortillas are soft and the filling is cooked through. Sprinkle with the remaining cheese and bake for about 5 minutes longer, or until the cheese is melted. Serve garnished with the sliced olives, if desired.

BEEF
with
BRAVADO

"For the sake of both our health and our budgets, I think we need to think of beef as a side dish."

Americans are in love with red meat, and the portion sizes that we've come to think of as "normal" have helped contribute to our problems with weight, cholesterol

levels, and budgets. I admit that I love a good steak as much as the next guy, but it's pretty sobering to realize that the giant steaks served in American steakhouses as individual portions would be considered enough to feed a family of six or more in many parts of the world, even in Western Europe.

For the sake of both our health and our budgets, I think we need to think of beef as a side dish. Not literally on the side, but proportionately. You might think a half-pound of steak and half-cup of vegetables is one serving, but 3 or 4 ounces of beef with several cups of vegetables is both healthier and a lot less expensive.

That's why you'll see that many of the beef recipes in this chapter are inspired by the cuisines of other countries, where people already know the relative importance of meat and vegetables. These recipes come from Mexico, Japan, France, Germany, Russia, and Greece, to name just a few.

STUFFED PEPPER JACK PEPPERS

Stuffed peppers should be a basic in any economical cook's repertoire. They have built-in "kid appeal"—children love things that come in single-serving portions, especially if you make smaller peppers just for them. As a friend's child said upon first seeing this dish, "It comes in its own house!"

I like using pepper Jack cheese—the spicier and less subtle sibling of Monterey Jack cheese—because of its built-in flavors and good melting consistency, but you can certainly substitute some mozzarella or Monterey Jack; just add ¼ teaspoon each of black and cayenne pepper to the recipe if you do. You can also make this recipe with ground turkey instead of beef.

4-6 ¢ SERVINGS

6   large green bell peppers
1   pound ground beef
2   tablespoons chopped onion
1   cup cooked brown rice
1   teaspoon garlic salt
1   teaspoon minced garlic
1   28-ounce can plum
      tomatoes, undrained
4   ounces shredded pepper
      Jack cheese (1 cup)

1. Preheat the oven to 350°F.
2. Slice off the tops of the peppers, discarding the seeds and caps. In a large pot, boil enough water to cover the peppers. Once it reaches a rolling boil, reduce the heat slightly and add the peppers. Gently boil the peppers until just tender but not soft, about 5 minutes. Drain the peppers and stand them upright in an 8 x 8-inch square baking dish.
3. Meanwhile, add the ground beef and onion to a nonstick skillet over medium-high heat. Cook, stirring to break up the meat, until the beef is cooked through, 5 to 7 minutes. Drain off any fat, then stir in the rice, garlic salt, and garlic.
4. Pour off the juice from the canned tomatoes into a bowl and set aside. Chop the drained tomatoes and add one-third to the skillet. Stir into the meat-and-rice mixture. Return the remaining chopped tomatoes to their liquid.
5. Stuff each pepper with the meat mixture, packing down lightly until the peppers are evenly filled. Pour the remaining chopped tomatoes, liquid and all, over the top of the peppers and cover the dish loosely with aluminum foil. Bake for about 30 minutes. Remove the foil cover and sprinkle the tops of the peppers with the shredded cheese. Bake until the cheese topping is melted, 7 to 10 minutes.

BEEF WITH PEA PODS

What's not to love about a stir-fry? The use of lots of veggies makes it filling and economical, and it cooks in a flash. Particularly when cooking with beef, it makes that recommended 3-ounce portion look like a lot more (in comparison to a 3-ounce steak or burger, which looks sort of miserly). Just make sure to do all your preparation first, so you can whiz through the cooking.

4 ¢ SERVINGS

- ¾ pound beef (chuck steak, top blade, or top round steak)
- 2 teaspoons cornstarch
- 1 teaspoon sugar
- ½ teaspoon salt
- ½ teaspoon freshly ground black pepper
- 2 tablespoons soy sauce
- 3 to 4 tablespoons canola oil
- 1 teaspoon minced garlic
- 1 teaspoon grated fresh ginger
- 2 pounds fresh snow peas, stemmed
- 1 8-ounce can sliced water chestnuts, drained
- 2 cups hot cooked white rice

1. Cut the steak into bite-size slices, about ¼ inch thick. Set aside.
2. In a small bowl, mix together the cornstarch, sugar, salt, and pepper. Blend in the soy sauce and ¼ cup water. Mix well with a wire whisk to remove any lumps.
3. Heat 2 tablespoons of the oil in a wok or large skillet over medium-high heat until a sprinkle of water causes it to "pop." Add the garlic and ginger and stir-fry until they begin to release fragrance, about 30 seconds. Add the snow peas and water chestnuts and cook, stirring, until the pea pods are crisp-tender, 1 to 2 minutes. Pour the mixture into a bowl and set aside.
4. Add another 1 or 2 tablespoons of oil to the wok—enough to coat the entire pan—and then add the beef. Cook, stirring, until it reaches the desired doneness, 1 to 3 minutes. Pour the soy sauce mixture into the pan, stir with a whisk, and then add the cooked vegetables. Cook, stirring, until the sauce thickens slightly, about 1 minute.
5. Serve over the rice.

TIPS >
To make slicing meat easier, chill it in the freezer until it feels firm, and use a nice big sharp knife.

HURRY-UP
MOUSSAKA

Moussaka is a classic Greek comfort food made with egg-plant and chopped beef. This Americanized version can be ready in a flash, more or less, and is a real budget-stretcher.

4 SERVINGS

1   **small eggplant (½ pound or so)**
½   **pound zucchini**
3   **tablespoons olive oil**
1   **small onion, sliced**
2   **tablespoons chopped fresh parsley**
1   **cup sliced white mushrooms**
1   **pound ground beef**
1   **6-ounce can tomato paste**
1   **teaspoon salt**
½   **teaspoon dried oregano**
4   **drops Tabasco sauce**
1   **cup milk**
4   **ounces shredded cheddar cheese (1 cup)**

1. Preheat the broiler.

2. Wash and dry the eggplant and the zucchini; do not peel. Cut the eggplant lengthwise into quarters, then cut it into ¼-inch slices. Cut the zucchini into ¼-inch slices.

3. Heat the oil in a large skillet over medium heat. Add the eggplant, zucchini, onion, and parsley and cook, covered, until tender, about 15 minutes. Stir in the mushrooms, reduce the heat to a simmer, and cook, uncovered, for 5 more minutes.

4. Meanwhile, in another large skillet, cook the ground beef over medium heat, breaking it up and stirring just until it is no longer red. Drain off the fat. Stir in the tomato paste, salt, oregano, and Tabasco. Cook, stirring, until hot and well blended, 3 to 4 minutes longer.

5. Meanwhile, heat the milk in a medium-size bowl in the microwave for 2 minutes, or until hot. Add the grated cheese to the milk and stir until it melts, microwaving for an additional 15 seconds at a time if necessary.

6. Lightly grease a round, shallow 2-quart baking dish. Arrange the vegetables around the perimeter and put the meat mixture in the center. Pour the cheese sauce over everything. Broil for 2 or 3 minutes, until lightly browned.

LEFTOVER-BEEF STROGANOFF

Make this easy beef dish with leftover rare roast beef, or you can use any beef sold for stir-fry. If you think you don't like sour cream—or that your children won't—never fear; it makes the sauce rich and tangy, but definitely not sour!

4 SERVINGS

2 tablespoons butter
½ pound leftover roast beef
1 package dried onion soup mix
1 10-ounce can sliced mushrooms, undrained
8 ounces egg noodles
16 ounces (1 pint) low-fat sour cream
1 tablespoon chopped fresh parsley

1. Melt 1 tablespoon of the butter in a large skillet over medium heat. Add the beef and cook, stirring occasionally, until browned. Stir in the onion soup mix. Add ½ cup water and the mushrooms, including their juice. Reduce the heat, cover, and simmer for 5 minutes.

2. Meanwhile, cook the noodles according to the package directions. When the noodles are done, drain them. Mix the sour cream into the meat mixture and stir until warm. Toss the noodles with the remaining 1 tablespoon butter and the parsley and serve the beef mixture on top.

SAUERBRATEN-BURGERS

Sauerbraten is a German pot roast made with vinegar that requires long, slow cooking, but this variation gives hamburgers a real upgrade. Use low-fat or fat-free gravy, which is much easier than trying to skim the gravy you make at home. This goes great with mashed potatoes and steamed carrots.

1   **pound ground beef**
1   **large egg, beaten**
¼   **cup bread crumbs**
½   **cup minced onion**
⅓   **cup milk**
1   **teaspoon salt**
½   **teaspoon grated lemon zest**
      Dash of freshly ground
         black pepper
1   **teaspoon butter**
1   **12-ounce can or jar low-fat**
         beef gravy
2   **tablespoons white wine**
         vinegar
¼   **cup lightly packed brown**
         sugar
½   **teaspoon ground ginger**
      Dash of ground cloves
1   **bay leaf**

1. In a large bowl, lightly mix together the beef, egg, bread crumbs, onion, milk, salt, lemon zest, and pepper. Shape the mixture with your hands into four large patties.

2. Melt the butter in a large skillet over medium heat. Add the patties and cook until browned on both sides. Remove the patties to a plate and drain off the fat from the skillet.

Add the gravy and vinegar to the skillet; stir and scrape up any bits from the bottom of the skillet. Add the brown sugar, ginger, cloves, and bay leaf and stir well. Bring to a boil.

3. Reduce the heat and return the patties to the skillet. Cover and simmer for 30 minutes, turning occasionally. Serve hot.

TIPS >
To make your own low-fat gravy, pour any homemade gravy into a heatproof glass container and refrigerate. Remove the fat layer that settles on the top.

BEEF BURGUNDY

Boeuf bourguignonne, as it's known in France, is a basic country stew. It has plenty of vegetables, but unlike the stews of other Western countries, no potatoes. You can serve it over noodles or with sautéed baby potatoes, and it's even better the second day. Red Burgundy wine is, of course, traditional, but any hearty dry red wine will do.

A good trick for coating the beef cubes is to put them into a paper bag along with the flour, close tightly, and shake.

4 ¢ SERVINGS

2 tablespoons butter
1 pound cubed lean beef
¼ cup all-purpose flour
4 large carrots, peeled, halved lengthwise, and cut into quarters
1 cup thinly sliced onion
1 cup thinly sliced celery
½ teaspoon minced garlic
1½ cups dry red wine
¾ cup beef broth
1 teaspoon salt
½ teaspoon dried thyme
2 bay leaves
½ pound white mushrooms, quartered or halved depending on size

1. Melt the butter in a Dutch oven or other heavy pot over medium heat. Coat the beef cubes with the flour. Brown the beef in the Dutch oven, turning occasionally so that all sides brown.

2. Stir in the carrots, onion, celery, and garlic. Pour the wine and broth into the pot, then add the salt, thyme, and bay leaves. Bring just to a boil, then reduce the heat and simmer for 2 hours, adding more broth and/or wine if necessary to maintain a thick sauce. Add the mushrooms and simmer for an additional 30 minutes. Serve hot.

BEEF UPSIDE-DOWN CASSEROLE

This is one of those standbys that kids seem to love because it gets turned upside-down. If you have hamburger meat and a few staples in the kitchen, you can put it together in a flash.

SERVINGS

1   tablespoon canola oil
1   cup sliced onion
½   pound ground beef
1   10.5-ounce can tomato
    puree
    Worcestershire sauce
1   11.5-ounce can refrigerator
    biscuits

1. Preheat the oven to 350°F.
2. Heat the oil in a medium-size skillet over medium heat. Add the onion and cook, stirring, until it is soft and golden, 2 to 3 minutes. Add the meat and cook, stirring and breaking it up, until browned. Pour in the tomato puree, add a dash or two of Worcestershire sauce, and stir well.

3. Scrape the contents of the skillet into a 2-quart baking dish. Place the refrigerator biscuits side by side over the top of the meat mixture. Bake for 10 to 15 minutes, until the biscuits are browned.
4. To serve, put a serving dish on top of the casserole and invert it, so that the biscuits are on the bottom.

SKINNY STEAK "FRITZ"

Steak frites is a classic French bistro meal—sort of the fast food of France and Belgium, until McDonald's came to town. It's just a skinny steak served with skinny french-fried potatoes (*frites*). Really good shoestring fries require a number of steps and high cooking-oil temperatures and are hard to make at home; a package of frozen oven-baked shoestring potatoes is a good substitute. Add a side salad and you're ready to go.

Because these steaks are traditionally skinny, this recipe can make nice cuts of steak affordable. You don't want them to be more than ½ inch thick, so if you like, you can buy a thick steak and slice it in half lengthwise (chill it first, which makes it easy to cut with a sharp knife). For a tasty steak that's less expensive than rib eye, try chuck eye. You can also substitute lemon juice for the red wine. The key ingredient is a large, heavy skillet.

4 SERVINGS $

Extra-virgin olive oil
4 **3- or 4-ounce boneless chuck-eye or rib-eye steaks, ½ inch thick**
1 **large shallot, minced**
2 **tablespoons butter**
2 **tablespoons red wine**

1. Lightly coat the surface of a large, heavy skillet with oil. Preheat over medium-high heat until very hot, at least 5 minutes. Add the steaks to the skillet and let cook for 3 minutes. Then flip them over and repeat on the other side. Cook longer if you prefer your steaks more well done. Remove the steaks to a plate and let them rest for at least 5 minutes.

2. Reduce the heat to low. Add the shallot to the skillet and cook, stirring, until softened, about 1 minute. Add the butter and raise the heat back to medium-high. Use a spatula to scrape the bottom of the skillet so that nothing is left stuck to the bottom. Watching carefully, stir in the wine; as soon as it is hot, pour over the steaks and serve.

TIPS >
To make slicing meat easier, chill it in the freezer until it feels firm, and use a nice big sharp knife.

STEAK FAJITAS

Although thanks to Mexican restaurants the term *fajitas* has come to mean any combination of marinated meat (or chicken, or even fish) cut into strips, grilled, served with onions and peppers, and wrapped in a flour tortilla, the name actually comes from a specific cut of beef, the *faja*, which is the strap muscle from a cow's diaphragm. Mexican cowboys working in Texas used to be given the cheapest, toughest cuts of meat to eat, so they would tenderize them and cook them over an open fire. Although better cuts of meat are used today, it's still the marinating that gives fajitas their tenderness and flavor. This recipe calls for broiling the meat; to grill it, add 2 tablespoons olive oil to the marinade, and don't slice the meat until after it's cooked. If you choose, you can substitute white vinegar for the beer. Salsa and guacamole are traditional condiments to serve with fajitas, but they aren't mandatory.

4-6 $ SERVINGS

½ cup lime juice
½ tablespoon ground cumin
1 teaspoon freshly ground black pepper
1 teaspoon cayenne pepper
1 teaspoon salt
2 teaspoons minced garlic
¼ cup beer
1 pound flank steak, round steak, or other flat cut of beef
1 teaspoon canola oil
1 red bell pepper, seeded and cut into long, narrow strips
1 green bell pepper, seeded and cut into long, narrow strips
1 large onion, cut into rings
8 flour tortillas
Salsa and guacamole, for serving (optional)

1. In a large bowl, mix together the lime juice, cumin, black pepper, cayenne, salt, and 1 teaspoon of the minced garlic. Stir in the beer.

2. Cut the meat lengthwise into 3 or 4 pieces and add to the bowl with the marinade. Cover and refrigerate for at least 30 minutes, and preferably overnight.

3. Preheat the broiler.

4. Drain the meat and discard the marinade. Broil the meat about 4 inches from the heat source for 5 to 6 minutes per side. Remove from the heat and slice into ¼-inch-thick strips; place on a platter.

5. Heat the canola oil in a large skillet or wok. Add the bell pepper, onion, and remaining 1 teaspoon garlic and cook, stirring, until barely softened, 2 to 3 minutes. Remove with a slotted spoon to the platter. Serve with warm tortillas and allow diners to assemble their own. Serve with salsa and/or guacamole on the side, if desired.

GRILLED STEAK SALAD

Serving steak in a salad has several advantages: It makes the meat go further, and it requires only a fairly lean cut of meat. When the steak is served hot, it really feels more like a meal. You can grill the meat and vegetables outdoors or indoors, or broil them.

SERVINGS 4–6 $

2 **large carrots, peeled and sliced on the long diagonal about ¼ inch thick**

2 **portobello mushroom caps, sliced ¼ inch thick**

1 **large onion, sliced ¼ inch thick**

1 **cup store-bought red wine vinaigrette**

1 **pound London broil or round steak, about 1½ inches thick**

1¼ **pounds mixed field greens**

2 **ounces crumbled blue cheese (optional)**

1. Preheat the grill or broiler.

2. Put the carrots, mushrooms, and onion in a large plastic bag. Add ¼ cup of the vinaigrette and shake to coat.

3. Grill or broil the meat for 4 to 5 minutes per side; it should still be rare. Remove from the heat and let it rest for 5 minutes for the juices to settle. Meanwhile, drain off the marinade from the vegetables and add them to the grill or broiler pan; discard the marinade. Grill the vegetables until tender but not limp, 3 to 4 minutes per side.

4. In a large salad bowl, toss the field greens with the remaining vinaigrette. Divide the salad equally among four or more plates. Top with the grilled vegetables. Thinly slice the steak and lay the slices over the tops of the salads. Sprinkle with blue cheese, if desired.

BEEF IN BEER

This is a variation on a traditional French country recipe called *carbonnade flamande*, which is essentially a stew cooked with beer. The long, slow cooking makes less expensive cuts of meat tender and tasty. Because it gets even better the second day, this makes enough for 8 servings, so you'll have leftovers. This is not a low-fat recipe and won't work very well with lean meat and turkey bacon, but if you prefer not to use the bacon fat, you can substitute 2 tablespoons olive oil. Serve this with crusty French bread.

8 ¢ SERVINGS

1	**2½- to 3-pound boneless chuck roast**
3	**large onions, quartered**
¼	**pound bacon**
3	**tablespoons butter**
2	**cups beer**
1	**cup beef broth**
3	**cloves garlic, chopped**
1	**tablespoon brown sugar**
½	**teaspoon dried thyme**
2	**bay leaves**
½	**teaspoon salt**
¼	**teaspoon freshly ground black pepper**
3	**1-inch slices of French bread, crusts removed**
3	**tablespoons Dijon mustard**
2	**tablespoons red wine vinegar**

1. Preheat the oven to 325°F.

2. Cut the meat into ¾-inch-thick slices. Cut each slice into 2 x 2-inch strips and set aside. Cut each quartered onion into ¼-inch-thick slices and set aside.

3. Cut the bacon into small pieces and place in a large skillet. Cook over medium heat until light brown and crisp. Transfer the bacon with a slotted spoon to a large, heavy heatproof casserole dish or Dutch oven.

4. Add the butter to the bacon fat in the skillet and increase the heat to high. Add one-quarter of the meat strips at a time and cook, stirring, until the meat is browned; transfer the meat to the casserole. Add the onions to the skillet and cook, stirring occasionally, until light brown, about 3 minutes. Transfer to the casserole.

5. Add the beer, broth, garlic, brown sugar, thyme, bay leaves, salt, and pepper to the casserole and stir.

6. Spread the bread on both sides with the mustard and place on top of the stew. Cover, place the casserole over a burner, and bring to a boil over medium-high heat. Transfer the casserole to the oven and cook for 1½ to 2 hours, until the meat is very tender.

7. Return the casserole to the stovetop over medium heat. Stir the vinegar into the dish and simmer for 2 minutes.

8. Pour off all the liquid into a saucepan and skim off the fat. Bring the liquid to a boil until it thickens to the consistency of gravy. Pour back over the meat, and serve directly from the pot.

TIPS >
To protect your surfaces when serving hot casseroles, you don't need to go out and buy trivets. Pretty pot holders from the dollar store or single tiles from the home-improvement center can be color-coordinated with your table setting and will do the trick!

PRACTICAL

PORK

"You can safely and healthfully add a nice range of pork recipes to your repertoire."

A lot of cultures developed inexpensive recipes around pork for the simple reason that it was much easier to raise a pig or two without having a farm or the large

grazing area needed to raise a cow. Other cultures developed taboos about pork, often for the simple reason that in warm climates the risk of trichinosis—a disease caused by a parasite found in pork—was high. Today, any common germs in pork can be killed by proper cooking; never eat pork rare.

Pork has also gotten a bad rap as being fatty. Certain cuts of pork do have quite a bit of fat, but any cut referring to "pork loin" is likely to be quite lean. Pork tenderloin, the leanest of all, has only about the same fat and calories ounce for ounce as chicken breast, while other loin cuts are about the same, fat-wise and calorie-wise, as chicken thigh.

I'll often cook a pork chop or pork steak, trimmed of fat and well seasoned, in a skillet without any oil over very low heat. As long as you don't let it dry out, that's all it needs. What gives pork its "fatty" reputation, really, is an American culinary tradition of frying pork chops in fat—that, and bacon, which is very fatty. If you watch the added fat when you're cooking pork, and cut back on bacon (or use the low-fat, turkey-based variety), you can safely and healthfully add a nice range of pork recipes to your repertoire.

Besides being readily available, often inexpensive, and frequently lean, another advantage to pork is that it goes well with fruit and various sauces—which can make it very tempting to kids, always an advantage for those of us whose children are going through that "finicky eater" stage. My son and I love to bake chops and top them off with a nice mango salsa or throw some sliced apples and onions in with them to cook.

Since you're probably not raising your own pig, it's wise to be aware of the wide range of prices on pork products. As we always suggest, be flexible with your shopping list and you're likely to find one cut of pork or another that's a really good buy at the market.

Whole pork tenderloins are great, and versatile, but often expensive; however, you can sometimes find them on sale, or they can be more affordable when purchased in bulk. If you see them for under $5 a pound, it's worth stocking up. They're boneless, all meat, and can be served as mini-roasts or sliced thin as a great substitute for veal cutlets.

Center-cut boneless pork loin is often priced under $3 a pound. You can ask your supermarket butcher to cut you just as much as you need—or cut it into meal-size portions when you get home and freeze the rest. We always suggest cutting your meat into meal-size portions because if you serve it all, people will probably consume more than an appropriate portion. Even if you cook a whole pork roast, cut off some for leftovers—large slices can substitute for pork chops in some recipes, and even the little pieces are great for making stir-fries.

You'll also often find pork chops for under $3 a pound. Look for thin ones; they'll be a more appropriate portion size and will cook both faster and more thoroughly. Pork chops, no matter their size, are essentially single-serving items, and you just don't need a big fat one!

Ham is another member of the pork family. Here we use the term to refer to the pink kind, which is actually smoked and salted pork. Smoked half-hams are usually the least expensive per pound, and sometimes you can find good deals on canned hams. Ham keeps well and has so many uses for breakfast, lunch, and dinner that it can be a good value as long as you don't get carried away with your portion sizes. Ham steaks can be a little too expensive; it's easy enough to cut slices off a larger ham rather than paying for the privilege of buying them already cut.

PEAR-GINGER PORK CHOPS WITH GRILLED PINEAPPLE

Pears and pork are a nice combination, especially when it's spiced up a little. For a more Asian flavor, you can substitute soy sauce or teriyaki sauce for the barbecue sauce in this recipe. Also, see the note that follows the recipe for alternatives to pear preserves. We like this with mashed potatoes, but you can use any starch you prefer.

4 SERVINGS $

¼   **cup chili powder**
1   **teaspoon minced garlic**
½   **teaspoon salt**
¼   **teaspoon freshly ground black pepper**
4   **thin, bone-in pork chops (about 1 pound)**
½   **cup pear preserves or jam**
½   **cup barbecue sauce**
1   **tablespoon chopped fresh parsley**
1   **tablespoon lime juice**
1   **teaspoon grated fresh ginger (or ¼ teaspoon ground ginger)**
1   **pound baby carrots**
1   **teaspoon butter or margarine (optional)**

1. Combine the chili powder, garlic, salt, and pepper in a small mixing bowl. Rub the spices into the pork chops and let sit, covered, in the refrigerator for at least 2 hours, or overnight. About 30 minutes before you're ready to cook, preheat the oven to 350°F.

2. In a small saucepan, combine the preserves, barbecue sauce, parsley, lime juice, and ginger. Cook over medium heat, stirring constantly, until well blended and smooth, about 2 minutes. Remove from the heat.

3. Place the pork chops in a lightly greased 9 x 13-inch baking dish. Bake for about 20 minutes, or until the pork is cooked through. During the last 5 minutes of baking, brush the pork with half of the glaze.

4. While the pork chops are cooking, combine the carrots with the butter or 1 tablespoon water and a dash of black pepper in a microwave-safe bowl. Cover and microwave until the carrots are just tender, 5 to 7 minutes.

5. Just prior to serving, reheat the remaining glaze and drizzle it over the pork.

Note: Pear preserves are sometimes found only in the "gourmet" section, priced accordingly. If you can't find an inexpensive version, you can easily make the glaze yourself from scratch. Just peel and chop 1 large pear and cook it in a skillet with a little butter over medium heat until lightly browned. Add ¼ cup water, 1 tablespoon brown sugar, 1 teaspoon lemon juice, and a dash of cinnamon. Boil until thickened, puree in a blender or mash with a fork, and use it instead of the preserves in the recipe. You can also substitute apple preserves or drained sweet applesauce.

CRANBERRY PORK WITH ROASTED RED POTATOES

Here's a fruity pork recipe that kids will love. Brown sugar gives it additional sweetness but also adds calories, so if you're watching your weight, sprinkle some brown sugar just over the top of the pot before you stick it in the oven, or use a brown-sugar substitute or low-calorie maple syrup instead. The pork can also be made in a slow cooker, on low for 6 to 8 hours.

4 SERVINGS **$**

4   lean, bone-in pork loin chops (about 1 pound)
     Salt and freshly ground black pepper
½   teaspoon grated orange zest
1   teaspoon ground cinnamon
1   16-ounce can jellied cranberry sauce
½   cup orange juice
1   tablespoon dark brown sugar (optional)

For Roasted Potatoes:
5   red potatoes, scrubbed and cubed
¼   cup chicken broth
2   tablespoons olive oil
2   tablespoons balsamic vinegar
1½   teaspoons minced garlic
⅓   teaspoon dried thyme
⅓   teaspoon dried rosemary, crumbled

1. Preheat the oven to 350°F.
2. Spray a skillet with a nonstick cooking spray and set over medium heat. Season the pork chops with a little salt and pepper. Add them to the skillet and cook until browned, about 2 minutes per side. Place the pork chops in a large covered baking dish or casserole dish and sprinkle with the orange zest and cinnamon.
3. In a medium-size bowl, combine the cranberry sauce, orange juice, and brown sugar, if desired, and stir together until well blended and smooth. Pour over the pork chops and bake for 30 minutes, or until the pork is thoroughly cooked.

4. As soon as you put the pork into the oven, prepare the roasted potatoes. Put the cubed potatoes in a medium-size oven- and microwave-safe dish with a splash of water and cook, uncovered, in the microwave on high for 3 minutes. Add the broth, oil, vinegar, garlic, thyme, and rosemary and stir to mix well. Put the pan in the oven alongside the pork and roast for about 25 minutes, or until the potatoes are tender.

TIPS >
If you're panfrying any meats—from hamburgers to chops to steak—in a dry pan, wait to add your salt and add it to the side you have already cooked. Salt draws the juices of meat to the surface, where contact with the hot pan will cause them to evaporate, leaving your meat dry.

MINI PORK ROAST
WITH RED CABBAGE AND PUMPERNICKEL GRAVY

4 SERVINGS **$**

This can be a nice meal for entertaining or for Sunday dinner because it really looks pretty when you arrange it on a platter. If you don't keep pumpernickel bread in the house, you don't have to go out and buy a whole loaf to make this; you can substitute rye bread, or just buy one pumpernickel roll. To make the bread "stale" fast, stick it in a 250°F oven for 10 minutes, until it feels a little dried out. You can also substitute 1 tablespoon minced onion for the shallot if you already have onions around. Another nice thing about this recipe is that you can make it entirely on top of the stove.

2 **tablespoons canola oil**

1 **pound pork tenderloin or boneless rolled pork loin, 2 to 3 inches in diameter**

3 **medium baking potatoes, peeled and cut into 1½-inch-thick slices**

1 **head red cabbage, cored and coarsely shredded**

2 **tablespoons butter or margarine**

¼ **teaspoon caraway seeds Salt and freshly ground black pepper**

1 **teaspoon mustard (brown or Dijon)**

1 **slice or roll stale pumpernickel bread**

1¼ **cups chicken broth**

1 **shallot, minced**

¼ **teaspoon minced garlic**

1. Heat the oil in a large Dutch oven or other heavy pot over medium heat until it ripples. Add the pork and cook, turning occasionally, until it's browned all over, about 10 minutes total. Reduce the heat to medium-low. Add the potato slices, scattering them around the pork. Cover and cook for 30 minutes, turning everything occasionally so that it's all evenly browned on all sides.

2. Meanwhile, in a large pot, bring about a quart of water to a boil. Add the cabbage and boil it for about 3 minutes; drain thoroughly and pat with a paper towel to remove excess water.

3. Melt the butter in a large skillet over medium heat. Add the drained cabbage and the caraway seeds to the skillet and cook, stirring occasionally, until the cabbage is tender, about 20 minutes. Season to taste with salt and a dash of pepper.

4. While the cabbage is cooking, spread the mustard on the bread (if using a roll, slice it first). Put the bread into a small pot and add the broth and ⅛ teaspoon pepper. Bring to a boil over medium heat. Let it cook down a little, whisking occasionally, so that you have about a cup of liquid remaining, about 3 minutes. Place in a blender or food processor and puree.

5. Cover the bottom of a platter with the cabbage to make a bed. Remove the pork and potatoes from the Dutch oven and arrange on the cabbage; cover with aluminum foil to retain the heat.

6. Pour off any excess fat from the Dutch oven, but leave a film of drippings in the pot. Add the shallot and garlic to the Dutch oven over medium heat and cook, stirring, for 1 minute. Scrape the bottom of the pan and add the pureed pumpernickel gravy. Bring to a boil, stirring constantly. Reduce the heat to very low, to keep warm.

7. When you're ready to serve, place the pork on a cutting board, slice it into about 1½-inch-thick slices, and arrange them down the center of the platter. Pour the gravy over the pork and potatoes.

FINGER-LICKIN' PULLED PORK
WITH BEANS AND CORN

This recipe needs long, slow cooking, so it's simplest to do it in an electric slow cooker. Otherwise, bake it, covered, in a low oven (300°F) for at least 5 hours, adding more liquid as necessary. The recipe is great with fresh corn, but if it's not in season, you can use frozen corn.

4 SERVINGS $

1   pound boneless pork butt or shoulder, visible fat trimmed
1   large Vidalia onion, finely chopped
1   12-ounce bottle mild chili sauce such as Heinz, or Louisiana-style chili sauce
⅓   cup plus 2 tablespoons firmly packed dark brown sugar
⅓   cup apple cider vinegar
1   tablespoon Worcestershire sauce
2   teaspoons minced garlic
1   tablespoon chili powder
1   teaspoon freshly ground black pepper
1   28-ounce can pork and beans
1   small onion, chopped (about ½ cup)
1   tablespoon mustard
1   tablespoon sugar
4   ears fresh corn, or equivalent amount of frozen corn on the cob

1. In the crock of a slow cooker, combine the pork, onion, chili sauce, ⅓ cup of the brown sugar, the vinegar, Worcestershire sauce, garlic, chili powder, and pepper, mixing well. Cover and cook on low until the pork falls apart when stirring, 10 hours or more. When the pork is extremely tender, remove it from the crock to a plate, shred it with a knife or fork, return the meat to the crock, and mix it well into the sauce.

2. About an hour before serving, preheat the oven to 350°F.

3. Lightly grease a 9 x 13 inch casserole dish. Add the pork and beans, the remaining 2 tablespoons brown sugar, the onion, and the mustard to the casserole, stirring to mix. Bake for about 45 minutes.

4. Meanwhile, in a large pot bring 4 quarts of water to a rolling boil over high heat. Stir in the sugar. Add the corn and immediately reduce the heat to medium-high. Boil until the kernels pop when pricked with a knife, about 5 minutes.

5. Serve the pork with the beans and corn.

YAMMY HAM WITH CORN PUDDING

This is an example of classic American home cooking, with a lot of sweet flavor that kids will love. It's an easy, tasty, casual meal that can be made equally well with leftover ham.

4 $
SERVINGS

1   **15.5-ounce can creamed corn**
1   **6-ounce can evaporated milk**
2   **large eggs**
2   **tablespoons sugar**
1   **tablespoon cornstarch**
1   **teaspoon salt**
    Pinch of freshly ground black pepper
4   **medium yams, peeled**
2   **8-ounce smoked ham steaks, or 4 thick slices canned ham**
1   **tablespoon butter or margarine**

1. Preheat the oven to 350°F.
2. Lightly spray an 8 x 8-inch square baking dish with nonstick cooking spray. In a large bowl, combine the corn, milk, eggs, sugar, cornstarch, salt, and pepper. Pour into the baking dish and bake for about 45 minutes, or until golden.
3. While the pudding is in the oven, poke the yams with a knife or fork. Place them in a pot with enough water to cover and bring to a rolling boil over high heat. Reduce the heat to a low boil and cook until a knife inserts easily into a yam, 20 to 25 minutes.
4. Heat the ham steaks in a large, lightly greased skillet, turning to heat evenly, 1 to 2 minutes per side depending on thickness.
5. Slice the yams lengthwise and top each with a dab of the butter. Serve the yams and ham with the corn pudding.

PORK AND APPLE PIE WITH POTATO CRUST

This is a simple, one-dish meal. Add some green veggies or a salad and you're ready to go. For an even easier pie crust, you can omit the potatoes, and in the last half-hour, top the dish with slices of bread that have had their crusts removed and been flattened with a rolling pin; overlap them to cover, and brush with the beaten egg.

4 SERVINGS $

4   large baking potatoes, peeled

1   large egg, beaten

1   pound boneless pork butt or shoulder, visible fat trimmed and cut into 1½-inch cubes

2   large apples, peeled, cored, and cut into 1-inch cubes

1   small onion, chopped

1   teaspoon ground sage

1   teaspoon salt

¼   teaspoon ground nutmeg
    Freshly ground black pepper

1   cup apple cider (or 1 cup apple juice plus 1 teaspoon vinegar)

2   tablespoons sugar (white or brown)

1. Preheat the oven to 350°F.

2. Spray a 9-inch pie pan with nonstick cooking spray. Using a sharp knife or mandoline, slice the potatoes very thinly lengthwise. Reserve one-third of the potato slices. Cover the bottom and sides of the pie pan with overlapping slices of the remaining potatoes until the pan is fully covered. Brush the top with about 1 tablespoon of the beaten egg and bake for about 10 minutes, or until lightly browned. Remove from oven and let cool slightly.

3. Combine the pork, apples, onion, sage, salt, nutmeg, and a few twists of freshly ground pepper in a large bowl and toss until the pork and apples are thoroughly coated. Spread the mixture evenly over the potato crust. Pour the apple cider over everything. Sprinkle with sugar (reduce to 1 tablespoon sugar if you're using apple juice). Cover with aluminum foil and bake for 45 minutes.

4. Carefully remove the pie from the oven. Top with overlapping slices of the remaining potato to completely cover the pie. Brush the top with 2 tablespoons of the beaten egg. Return to the oven for another 45 minutes, brushing the top about halfway through with any remaining egg. Continue cooking as necessary until the top is browned.

5. Remove the pie from the oven and let it sit for 10 minutes to settle. Cut into slices to serve.

CILANTRO, PEPPERS, AND PORK
ASIAN TREAT

[4 SERVINGS $]

My friend Bill Rodgers, who devised this recipe, has been cooking since he was 10 years old and first saw Julia Child on TV. Bill pays attention to the visual appeal of this dish by cutting the meat and vegetables into a variety of different slices and chunks—some long and thin, some larger and square. When you cook, add the large pieces first so that everything cooks to the same degree of doneness. Bill also recommends using the "Chinese slicing" technique for the onion: After you peel the onion, cut a thin slice from the bottom so it stands up. Take turns cutting slices from each side of the onion as if you were making it into a square, and keep turning it as you slice so that you are always cutting the largest possible slice. It's also much easier to slice the pork (or any meat) if you chill it briefly in the freezer until it's slightly firm to the touch.

1 **pound lean, boneless pork loin, visible fat trimmed**
2 **medium bell peppers (in color of choice)**
2 **cups fresh snow peas**
1 **or 2 bunches fresh cilantro**
½ **cup soy sauce**
2 **tablespoons dark brown sugar**
4 **teaspoons cornstarch**
1 **teaspoon sesame oil (optional)**
  Up to ½ cup peanut or vegetable oil
1 **large sweet onion, sliced**
8 **to 10 garlic cloves, chopped**
1 **8-ounce can sliced water chestnuts, drained (optional)**
2 **cups hot cooked white rice**

1. Slice the pork into thick (about ½-inch wide) and thin (about ¼-inch wide) strips, all about 2 inches long. Slice and chop the bell peppers into a variety of different-size slices and chunks—some long thin slices, some larger square cuts—for visual appeal. Pull the stems from the snow peas to remove the "strings." Remove the stems from the cilantro and finely chop the leaves.

2. In a mixing bowl, combine the soy sauce, brown sugar, and cornstarch with 1 cup water. Add the sesame oil, if desired. Set aside.

3. Heat a wok or large frying pan until very hot. Add ¼ cup of the peanut oil, swishing it around to cover the bottom of the pan and being careful not to let it burn; turn the heat down to medium. Add the pork to the wok, larger pieces first, then the smaller pieces, and about one-third of the cilantro.

Cook, stirring, until the pork is well browned—up to 4 minutes for the largest pieces. Using a slotted spoon, remove the pork to a plate.

4. Turn the heat back up to high until you start to see some steam, or the pan juices start to sizzle. Add more oil if needed. Stir in the snow peas and about 2 tablespoons water for a cloud of steam. Add the onion, garlic, and the remaining cilantro, stirring after each addition. Mix in the water chestnuts, if desired.

5. Reduce the heat to medium and stir in the peppers, larger pieces first, then the smaller pieces. Return the pork to the wok. Give the soy sauce mixture a quick stir, then slowly pour it into the wok. Reduce the heat to medium-low and stir until the sauce begins to thicken, 1 to 2 minutes.

6. Serve in bowls over the rice.

OLD SOUTH PORK CHOPS AND COLLARD GREENS

This is real Southern home cooking. If you can't find or don't like fresh collard greens, you can substitute frozen greens, or try fresh turnip greens, fresh kale, or (less Southern) fresh spinach. Also, if you must, you can substitute salt pork for the ham hocks.

SERVINGS

2   **large or 3 small smoked ham hocks**
2   **10.5-ounce cans low-sodium chicken broth**
1   **tablespoon dark brown sugar**
1   **tablespoon white vinegar**
1½ **teaspoons minced garlic**
¼   **teaspoon freshly ground black pepper**
2   **large egg whites**
1   **cup cornmeal**
4   **6-ounce bone-in pork chops**
1   **bunch collard greens, stems trimmed and chopped**

1. Add the ham hocks, broth, brown sugar, vinegar, garlic, and pepper to a large pot. Add 3 cups water, mix well, and bring to a boil over high heat. Reduce the heat to medium, cover, and simmer until the meat falls off the bones, about 2 hours.

2. While the stock is cooking, preheat the oven to 350°F.

3. About 30 minutes before serving time, beat the egg whites in a shallow bowl. Shake the cornmeal onto a shallow plate. Brush the pork chops with the egg whites, then pat each side of the pork chop in the cornmeal to coat. Place the pork chops in a lightly greased 9 x 13-inch baking pan. Bake for about 25 minutes, or until the pork is cooked through.

4. While the pork is baking, use a slotted spoon to scoop out the ham hocks and any bone fragments from the pot. Scrape any meat off of the bones and add it back to the pot. Add the collard greens, cover, and simmer until they are wilted and tender, about 10 minutes.

5. Remove the collard greens and ham bits from the pot with a slotted spoon and serve alongside the pork chops.

TIPS >
Any clean brush can be used for coating or basting, including basting brushes, bottle brushes, and paintbrushes. Dollar stores are a good source. Just be sure to sterilize between uses, and discard when the brush begins shedding bristles.

other
MARVELOUS
MEATS

"If you rule out one meat, either because you can't find it or because it's too expensive, try the recipe with another."

I know, "other" seems like a cop-out category. But really, this is about versatility. Some of these recipes call for sausage, and you might think, why isn't that in the pork

section? Aha—because sausage doesn't have to be made of pork. It can be made from beef, or good-for-you turkey, or a mixture of several different meats. It can even be vegetarian. Different countries have their signature sausage, and they're all worth trying, but feel free to substitute your own favorite sausage and see how it works.

There are quite a few lamb recipes here as well. I love lamb. It has a special flavor all its own and it cooks great, but it can also be pricey. Most American recipes call for lamb roasts or lamb chops, which are the most expensive cuts, while many other countries' recipes call for cubed, sliced, or chopped lamb to make smaller amounts of lamb go further, and that's a valuable lesson.

Some of the lamb recipes in this chapter didn't start out calling for lamb, either. We've adapted them to use lamb instead of the specialty meats that might be more traditional and common in another country but aren't exactly found in every

supermarket here. For example, my mom is from Jamaica, and the real special-occasion roast there is goat. I grew up in New York, so my first time eating goat was when I went to Jamaica to see my uncle Bob Marley's family. Lo and behold, to celebrate our visit they strung up a goat. I said to myself, no way am I going to eat that cute little goat, but of course I love it now and eat it any chance I get. The Jamaican way, with the curry and the rice and peas, is my favorite, but in general goat is very good-tasting, easy to cook with, and very lean. If you don't believe me, check it out at your local West Indian restaurant.

While traveling around, I hear a lot of stories from people who are encountering meats that used to be considered unusual. A friend went to a holiday party right here in the U.S. of A., and the main course was rabbit. She thought it was pretty brave of the hostess to serve it, but she loved it. You can use rabbit in many chicken recipes, actually, especially those that use red wine.

Other people I meet are coming across unusual meats during their own travels—goat at a banquet in Switzerland, antelope in South Africa. While they may not be running home and saying "Gotta get me some antelope!" they are saying, I want that recipe; let's see how I can make it work with the meat I can buy at the local supermarket.

So this chapter is about broadening your horizons. If you rule out one meat, either because you can't find it or because it's too expensive, try the recipe with another, or even with turkey or something soy-based. The bigger your recipe repertoire, the better the chances you can keep control of your purse strings when you go shopping. I want you to learn what you can do with one meat that's on sale, or with a small amount of another. Having a limited budget doesn't limit your options, once you season them with creativity.

BANANA PEPPERS
AND SAUSAGE MARINARA

Banana peppers look pretty much like they sound, and they make a nice change from green bell peppers when you're looking for something to stuff. My friend Lisa Vernon, who "designed" this recipe, has two school-age children and likes to create meals that look as good as they taste.

A useful tip: Younger banana peppers tend to be paler, smaller, and milder; older, brightly colored banana peppers are larger and easier to stuff, but also hotter, so be cautious if you don't have a high tolerance for spicy food. You can, of course, simply substitute medium-size bell peppers for the banana peppers in this recipe. Similarly, you can use either sweet or hot sausage, depending upon personal preference.

4 ¢ SERVINGS

1   tablespoon olive oil
1   28-ounce can diced tomatoes
4   to 5 cloves garlic, crushed
⅛   teaspoon salt
    Freshly ground black pepper
¾   pound sweet or hot bulk Italian sausage
4   large banana peppers (see headnote)
4   ounces shredded mozzarella cheese (1 cup)
8   ounces spaghetti, cooked, drained, and kept warm

1. Preheat the oven to 350°F.
2. In a large skillet over medium heat, warm the oil, then add the tomatoes, garlic, salt, and several grinds of pepper, stirring occasionally, until the flavors are well blended, about 5 minutes. Keep warm. In another skillet over medium-high heat, crumble the sausage and cook, stirring, until browned, 3 to 4 minutes.
3. To prepare the peppers, remove the stems. Slice open one side of each pepper lengthwise and remove the seeds. Stuff the peppers with the sausage meat.

4. Place the stuffed peppers into a 9 x 13-inch baking dish and spoon a small amount of tomato mixture onto each pepper (reserve most of the sauce for serving). Cover the pan with aluminum foil and bake for 45 minutes. Remove the foil cover, sprinkle each pepper with one-quarter of the mozzarella, close the oven door, and turn off the heat. Remove from the oven once the cheese is melted, 5 minutes or less.
5. To serve, set the peppers on top of the spaghetti and spoon the reserved tomato sauce on top.

 + +

TIPS >

Whenever you are baking something in the oven for at least 30 minutes, it's a great opportunity to roast some vegetables. Celery, onion, carrots, and garlic are a good start; spread them in a single layer in a baking dish or pie pan with a small splash of olive oil and roast until tender. Add other (non-leafy) vegetables as desired. If you won't be using them within a day or two, you can freeze them in a plastic bag and reheat them in the microwave.

MOM'S JAMAICAN CURRY
WITH DUMPLINGS, RICE, AND PEAS

4 $ SERVINGS

My mother, Constance Marley, was born on the beautiful island of Jamaica. One of her favorite meals is curried goat with "rice and peas" and boiled dumplings, a meal that can be found on many West Indian tables around her hometown of Kingston, Jamaica. The "peas" in this recipe are actually beans, referred to as peas in Jamaica and throughout the Caribbean.

Goat curry was traditionally a meal for weddings and celebrations in Jamaica, but it has become a Sunday-dinner staple. Goat is a healthy, low-fat meat, so don't dismiss this recipe just because you haven't seen it in the supermarket lately! I've adapted it here using mutton.

2 tablespoons canola oil
1 pound boneless mutton, cut into 1-inch cubes
2 large onions, thinly sliced
1 14.5-ounce can vegetable broth
1 tablespoon red or white wine vinegar
1 tablespoon curry powder
1 teaspoon allspice
1 bay leaf

For Rice and Peas:
1 15-ounce can red kidney beans, undrained
1 13.5-ounce can coconut milk, shaken well
1 small onion, chopped
1 teaspoon minced garlic
1 teaspoon butter or margarine
2 cups long-grain rice
1 Scotch bonnet chile

1 tablespoon bottled jerk sauce

1. In a large skillet over medium heat, warm the oil, then add the meat and cook until browned on all sides. Remove the meat to a plate.
2. Add the onions to the oil in the skillet and cook, stirring, until softened, 1 to 2 minutes. Stir in the broth, vinegar, curry powder, and allspice. Return the meat to the skillet, add the bay leaf, cover, and simmer over medium-low heat for 2 hours.
3. About a half-hour before the meat will be done, make the rice and peas.

Combine the beans with their liquid, the coconut milk, onion, garlic, and butter with ½ cup water in a large skillet. Bring to a boil over medium heat, then stir in the rice. Reduce the heat to medium-low, place the whole Scotch bonnet chile on top of the liquid, cover lightly, and cook until the rice is ready, about 30 minutes. Discard the chile before serving.
4. When the meat is done, stir the jerk sauce into the curry. Adjust the seasonings to taste and serve with the rice and peas.

PERSIAN LAMB WITH DRIED FRUITS AND LENTILS

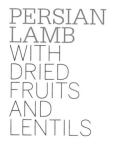

SERVINGS

This is a variation of the traditional Iranian dish *adas polow*. Because it is typically made with saffron, the rice has a yellow color; if saffron isn't handy, you can substitute long-grain yellow rice. Ground beef or chopped chicken can also be used in place of the lamb. You can substitute 3 ounces dried dates for the fresh dates, because their taste is stronger; if dates aren't handy, use figs or more raisins. The original dish gets extra texture from soaking basmati rice in water for several hours before cooking, but we soak it for only half an hour in our version. Also traditional is serving it in a mound—sort of a dome shape—on a platter.

16 ounces long-grain white rice (preferably basmati)
1   teaspoon salt
12 ounces dried lentils, rinsed
2   tablespoons canola oil
1   large onion, sliced
¾   pound boneless lamb, diced or minced
    Freshly ground black pepper
¼   pound fresh dates, pitted
1   cup raisins
½   teaspoon saffron

1. Wash and rinse the rice, then set it in a bowl to soak with enough water to cover for at least 30 minutes. Drain the rice, then transfer it to a nonstick pot with 4 cups fresh water and the salt. Bring just to a boil, then reduce the heat to medium, cover, and cook until the grains are just soft, 10 to 15 minutes. Drain again and set aside.

2. Meanwhile, in a medium-size pot, bring 2 to 3 cups water to a boil. Add the lentils and cook over medium heat until tender, 15 to 20 minutes.

3. In a large skillet over medium heat, warm 1 tablespoon of the oil. Add the onion and cook, stirring, until slightly golden, 1 to 2 minutes. Add the lamb and season with salt and pepper. Cook, stirring occasionally, until the meat is cooked through, about 10 minutes. Add 1 cup hot water and cook until the water has been mostly absorbed.

4. Remove the rice from its pot. Add ½ cup water and the remaining 1 tablespoon oil to the pot. Stir half of the rice back into the pot. Top with the lamb, lentils, dates, and raisins. Then add in the remaining rice, without stirring. Cook, covered, over low heat for about 20 minutes. While that's cooking, dissolve the saffron in ⅓ cup hot water. Just before serving, pour the saffron water over the rice and stir the whole pot well.

SAUERKRAUT SAUSAGE BAKE

Here's a recipe that draws on German comfort foods for a simple and attractive casserole that's a change of pace and easy on the budget too.

4-6 ¢ SERVINGS

8   **ounces egg noodles**
1   **pound German-style sausage links**
8   **ounces low-fat sour cream**
1   **16-ounce can sauerkraut, drained**
½   **cup milk**
1   **tablespoon butter or margarine, softened**
1   **tablespoon caraway seeds**
1   **teaspoon onion salt**
½   **teaspoon salt**
¼   **teaspoon freshly ground black pepper**

1. Preheat the oven to 375°F.

2. Cook the noodles according to the package directions and drain. Set aside.

3. Set a large nonstick skillet over medium-high heat and add enough water to cover the bottom to a depth of ¼ inch. Bring to a boil. Prick each of the sausages several times with a fork and cook in the boiling water for 5 minutes. Pour off the water and any accumulated fat, and brown the sausages in the hot pan for 5 more minutes, turning so they brown evenly.

4. While the sausages are cooking, add the sour cream to a 2-quart covered baking dish. Add the sauerkraut, milk, butter, caraway seeds, onion salt, salt, and pepper, stirring to blend. Add the noodles and stir well. Arrange the sausages, pinwheel style, on top of the noodles. Cover and bake for 30 minutes, until the sausages are thoroughly cooked all the way through and the various flavors have "married."

5. Slice or scoop to serve.

TIPS >

Whenever you are baking something in the oven for at least 30 minutes, it's a great opportunity to roast some vegetables. Celery, onion, carrots, and garlic are a good start; spread them in a single layer in a baking dish or pie pan with a small splash of olive oil and roast until tender. Add other (non-leafy) vegetables as desired. If you won't be using them within a day or two, you can freeze them in a plastic bag and reheat them in the microwave.

FRUITY LAMB CURRY

Curry and lamb go well together, and so do curry and fruit, so why not put them all together for this sure people-pleaser? If your market doesn't regularly sell lamb for stew, just ask the folks in the meat department to set aside some for you the next time they are butchering the more expensive cuts.

4 SERVINGS $

3 tablespoons curry powder
2 tablespoons all-purpose flour
1 teaspoon salt
1 pound lean lamb, cubed
2 tablespoons butter
1 tablespoon canola oil
1 medium onion, sliced
1½ cups chicken broth
   Juice of 3 lemons
1 green apple, peeled and cored
1 banana
1 8.5-ounce can pineapple chunks, drained
½ cup peach or mango chutney (optional)
2 cups hot cooked white rice

1. In a large bowl, combine the curry powder with 1 tablespoon of the flour and the salt. Mix thoroughly. Add the lamb cubes to the bowl and toss until they are thoroughly coated.

2. Heat the butter and oil together in a large skillet over high heat. Add the lamb and cook, turning to brown all sides, for about 10 minutes. Add the onion to the pan and cook, stirring, until it begins to soften, about 1 minute. Stir the remaining 1 tablespoon flour into the fat in the pan, stirring to brown. Add the chicken broth and lemon juice, reduce the heat, stir well, and simmer for 5 minutes.

3. Meanwhile, cut the apple into ½-inch cubes. Peel the banana and cut into 1-inch chunks. Add the apple, banana, pineapple, and chutney, if desired, to the skillet. Raise the heat and boil briefly.

4. Ladle the lamb curry and sauce over the rice.

SPANISH SAUSAGE WITH PLANTAINS

Here's a nice spicy-but-sweet dish that's a taste treat (but not for those watching their weight). Spanish chorizo, which this recipe calls for, doesn't need to be cooked; you can substitute pepperoni or kielbasa. Mexican chorizo is quite different and requires precooking.

4 ¢
SERVINGS

¾   **pound smoked chorizo (Spanish pork sausage)**
1   **small onion, minced**
1   **green bell pepper, seeded and chopped**
1   **teaspoon minced garlic**
1   **jalapeño chile, seeded and minced**
2   **cups cooked white rice**
1   **15-ounce can black beans, rinsed and drained**
1   **bunch fresh cilantro, stems discarded and leaves chopped**
1   **tablespoon Worcestershire sauce**
¼   **cup olive oil**
2   **ripe plantains, peeled and sliced ½ inch thick**
½   **cup firmly packed light brown sugar**
4   **soft corn tortillas, warmed**

1. In a large nonstick skillet over medium-high heat, brown the chorizo. Add the onion, bell pepper, garlic, and jalapeño. Cook over low heat, stirring constantly, until the vegetables are tender. Stir in the rice, beans, cilantro, and Worcestershire sauce.
2. In a second large skillet over medium-high heat, heat the oil until hot, then add the plantains and cook until golden, about 3 minutes per side. Transfer to a paper-towel-lined plate to absorb excess oil. Drain the oil from the skillet and reduce the heat slightly. Add the brown sugar and ½ cup water, stirring constantly until the sugar is dissolved and the mixture is syrupy. Return the plantains to the skillet, stirring thoroughly to coat. Cook, stirring, for 1 minute.
3. Transfer the sausage and rice mixture to a serving platter. Serve with the fried plantains and warm tortillas.

PERSONAL LAMB ROASTS

Lamb shanks are usually (but not always) less expensive than other cuts of lamb; save this recipe for when you find a good price on them. Cooking in liquid over low heat increases their tenderness. Serve with the vegetables that roast alongside the lamb and some mashed potatoes.

4 SERVINGS **$$**

- 4 lamb shanks (12 to 16 ounces total)
- 2 tablespoons olive oil
- 2 tablespoons all-purpose flour
- 1 teaspoon salt
  Freshly ground black pepper
- 1 cup beef broth
- 1 cup red wine
- 2 tablespoons tomato paste
- 1 clove garlic, crushed
- ⅛ teaspoon dried thyme, or 1 sprig fresh thyme
- 1 bay leaf
- 4 carrots, peeled and cut into chunks
- 2 teaspoons butter
- 1 pound button mushrooms, stems trimmed

1. Trim any excess fat and obvious tendons from the lamb shanks. Heat the oil in a heavy pot over medium-high heat. Sprinkle the lamb with the flour, salt, and a generous grinding of pepper. Add the lamb to the pot and cook, turning to brown evenly. Remove the lamb from the pot and set aside.

2. Pour out and discard the oil from the pot and add the broth and the wine. Raise the heat to high, bring to a boil, and then reduce the heat to simmer. Add the tomato paste, garlic, thyme, and bay leaf. Return the meat to the pot, cover, and simmer over low heat for 1 hour. Add the carrots to the pot and simmer for 20 minutes more.

3. Meanwhile, in a small skillet over medium heat, melt the butter, then add the mushrooms and cook, stirring, until they release their liquid, 3 to 5 minutes.

4. Just before serving, stir the mushrooms into the pot. Serve the individual lamb "roasts" with the braised vegetables. Pour the sauce over the lamb and vegetables.

SUBURBAN SHEPHERD'S PIE

Shepherds of old devised shepherd's pie to use up odd bits of lamb. Our "suburban" version is also designed to use leftovers—and lest you forget, having a plan to use all the leftover bits of a roast brings down its overall cost, too! This even uses leftover gravy and mashed potatoes. While we usually suggest using fresh vegetables whenever possible, frozen peas tend to be more consistently sweet and hold up better to cooking in mixtures with other ingredients.

4 ¢ SERVINGS

1 tablespoon olive oil
½ cup chopped onion
1 teaspoon minced garlic
½ teaspoon salt
¼ teaspoon freshly ground black pepper
2 cups diced leftover cooked lamb
1 10.5-ounce package frozen baby peas, thawed
3 cups hot leftover mashed potatoes
1 cup leftover lamb gravy
1 tablespoon melted butter

1. Preheat the oven to 350°F.

2. Heat the oil in a large skillet over medium heat. Add the onion and garlic and cook, stirring, until softened and fragrant, about 5 minutes. Add the salt and pepper and stir well. Add the lamb to the skillet and reduce the heat to medium-low. Stir the lamb until it is coated with the seasonings. Add the peas and cook for about 2 minutes; the peas should still be firm. Remove from the heat.

3. Spread half of the mashed potatoes evenly around the bottom of a lightly greased 2-quart baking dish. Pour the contents of the skillet over the potatoes and smooth lightly into an even layer. Pour the gravy on top of the lamb and peas. Top with the remaining potatoes.

4. Brush the top of the potatoes with the melted butter. Bake, uncovered, for 20 minutes, or until the top of the potatoes browns lightly.

5. Scoop to serve.

> The bigger your recipe repertoire, the better the chances you can keep control of your purse strings when you go shopping.

DIRTY RICE WITH SAUSAGE

This is a classic Cajun home-style recipe that is traditionally made with chicken gizzards, but if you don't have any gizzards handy—or just don't like the idea—you can substitute 1 cup of nuts (peanuts or, for a splurge, pine nuts) and add them with the onion. Use spicy smoked sausage, ideally Cajun andouille sausage if you can, but you can substitute kielbasa or even hamburger meat for the sausage.

6 SERVINGS

2   **cups chicken livers and gizzards**

½   **pound smoked sausage**

3   **tablespoons corn oil**

½   **cup chopped onion**

1   **green bell pepper, seeded and chopped**

½   **cup chopped celery**

2   **scallions, chopped (white and light green parts only)**

1   **clove garlic, chopped**

½   **teaspoon salt**

½   **teaspoon freshly ground black pepper**

4   **cups cooked white rice**

1. Add the chicken livers and gizzards to a saucepan with enough water to cover. Bring to a simmer, then cook over medium heat for 10 minutes. Drain the livers and gizzards and chop them.

2. Meanwhile, in a large skillet over medium heat, add the sausage and cook, stirring to break up the meat, until is well browned. (Hard sausage such as andouille will need to be chopped before cooking.) Transfer the meat to a plate, and drain off the fat.

3. Add the oil to the drained skillet. Put it back over medium heat and add the chicken livers and gizzards, onion, bell pepper, celery, scallions, garlic, salt, and black pepper. Cook, stirring, until the vegetables have softened, about 15 minutes. Stir in the cooked rice and continue to cook, stirring occasionally, for 5 minutes more. Serve hot.

PASTA

PRODIGIES

"One of the great things about pasta is that you can use whatever you have in the fridge."

Pasta is a Poor Chef favorite. If you're on a budget, pasta can make it go a long way. One of the great things about pasta is that you can use whatever you have in the fridge

or kitchen cabinets to make a good meal. Think about it: Start with a package of pasta that you can get for under a dollar, add some cut-up sausage, chicken, or chopped meat, season it with some simple spices, and you have a perfectly good meal.

And kids love pasta. I remember when I was growing up on Long Island, my best friend was from Haiti. He used to boil pasta, then drain it, add a small amount of oil to a pan, and almost sear the pasta for about 4 minutes. We would add franks, or whatever we might have, and some ketchup and we felt like kings. Pasta isn't an intimidating food.

All of those different names and shapes of pasta use basically the same recipe; what you pick just depends on what shapes you prefer, and how well you want it to hold the sauce. Just remember not to overcook your pasta and to drain it well before adding the sauce, and you're ahead of the game.

Also keep in mind that "sauce" can really be anything you put on top of the pasta, so take a break from tomato sauce and cream sauces from time to time; simple sautéed vegetables can make a great pasta topping too.

> Having a limited budget doesn't limit your options, once you season them with creativity.

BOW-TIE PARMESAN PASTA WITH CHICKEN

Alyssa Alonso appeared on my show in Tampa when she was 13, demonstrating this recipe. You can also make it with leftover chicken and try it with different pasta shapes.

4 ¢ SERVINGS

12 ounces bow-tie pasta

¼ cup olive oil, plus extra for the pasta

2 boneless, skinless chicken breast halves, chopped into 1-inch squares, or 2 cups cubed leftover cooked chicken

1 tablespoon minced garlic

½ teaspoon salt

¼ teaspoon freshly ground black pepper

1 large fresh tomato, chopped

¼ cup chopped fresh basil

¼ cup chopped scallion (white and light green parts only)

½ cup freshly grated Parmesan cheese

1. Cook the pasta according to the package directions. Drain and toss with a little olive oil to keep it from sticking together, and cover to keep warm. Set aside.

2. Add the ¼ cup oil to a large skillet over medium heat, heating until it shimmers. Stir in the uncooked chicken, garlic, salt, and pepper and cook, stirring frequently, until the chicken is no longer pink inside, 3 to 5 minutes.

3. Add the tomato, basil, and scallion to the skillet. (If using leftover chicken, add it here.) Continue to cook, stirring, until the chicken is hot and cooked through, 1 or 2 more minutes. Remove from the heat.

4. Add the drained pasta to a large serving bowl. Add the chicken mixture to the pasta and stir well. Gradually stir in the Parmesan.

HEALTHY TURKEY LASAGNA

If you're watching your cholesterol or just don't want to serve your family a lot of fatty food, it's easy to make lasagna with a lot less of the hidden fat than the traditional recipe has. We've used ground turkey to make this really lean, but you can make it with well-drained lean ground beef if you prefer. There is no need to cook the lasagna noodles separately; they will cook in the sauce. Also, if you find a good buy on larger containers of cheese, you can easily double the recipe and make two pans of lasagna; cool and then freeze the extra one for use at a later date.

4-6 $ SERVINGS

Olive oil or cooking spray
1 pound lean ground turkey
1 32-ounce jar thick spaghetti sauce
1 15-ounce container low-fat ricotta cheese
8 ounces shredded low-fat mozzarella cheese (1 cup)
½ cup freshly grated Parmesan cheese
2 large eggs
¼ cup chopped fresh parsley
1 teaspoon salt
½ teaspoon freshly ground black pepper
9 uncooked lasagna noodles

1. Preheat the oven to 350°F.

2. Lightly coat a large nonstick skillet with oil or cooking spray and set it over medium heat. Add the turkey and cook, breaking it up and stirring, until the meat is no longer pink, about 5 minutes. Add the spaghetti sauce and 1½ cups water to the skillet, reduce the heat, and simmer for about 10 minutes.

3. While the sauce is cooking, in a medium-size bowl combine the ricotta, mozzarella, Parmesan, eggs, parsley, salt, and pepper.

4. Pour 1 cup of the spaghetti sauce over the bottom of a 9 x 13-inch baking dish, spreading it evenly. Lay 3 lasagna noodles over the sauce to form the bottom layer. Cover the lasagna with 1 cup of the sauce. Spread half of the cheese mixture on top, to evenly cover the sauce layer. Repeat with a layer of 3 lasagna noodles, followed by half of the remaining sauce and then the rest of the cheese mixture. Top with the last 3 lasagna noodles and then the remainder of the sauce. Cover with aluminum foil.

5. Bake for 45 minutes. Remove from the oven and let settle for at least 10 minutes before cutting to serve.

LISA'S PORTOBELLO-FETA PASTA

My friend Lisa Vernon says that the idea for this recipe came from cajoling her husband into eating mushrooms. She originally designed this as an appetizer for her meat-and-potatoes man, and it was such a hit that she turned it into a main course.

If the portobello caps you find are really large—larger than the palm of your hand—you can use fewer of them and cut them in half before serving. And since portobellos are just giant cremini (aka baby bella) mushrooms, you can substitute cremini in a pinch.

Olives and feta give this a bit of a Greek flavor, but feel free to omit the olives and substitute mozzarella or Parmesan.

4 SERVINGS $

- **1** tablespoon olive oil, plus extra for the pasta and mushrooms
- **2** pounds tomatoes, seeded and chopped, or one 28-ounce can diced tomatoes, drained
- **4 to 5** cloves garlic, chopped
- **8** ounces angel-hair pasta
- **4** large portobello mushroom caps (each about the size of the palm of your hand)
- **4** ounces feta cheese
- **3** ounces black olives, sliced (optional)
- **1** tablespoon chopped fresh parsley

1. Preheat the oven to 350°F.

2. Heat the 1 tablespoon olive oil in a skillet over medium heat. Add the tomatoes and garlic and cook, stirring, until the flavors are well blended, 10 to 15 minutes.

3. Meanwhile, cook the pasta according to the package directions. Drain and toss with a little olive oil to keep it from sticking together, and cover to keep warm. Set aside.

4. While the tomatoes are cooking, or ahead of time, clean the portobellos: Carefully remove the gills and stems. Brush off any dirt with a paper towel. Brush each portobello cap, inside and out, with olive oil, and place cap-side down on a metal baking sheet. Using no more than half of the tomato mixture, spoon some into each portobello cap to fill. Sprinkle each filled cap with a small amount of feta cheese, reserving the rest. Bake until the cheese is slightly golden brown, 10 to 15 minutes.

5. Place the pasta on a serving dish and arrange the baked portobellos on top. Pour the remaining tomato mixture over the whole thing, and sprinkle with the rest of the feta cheese. Garnish with the sliced olives, if desired, and the parsley.

TIPS >
When using fresh mushrooms, brush off the dirt with a paper towel. Don't rinse them! Water dilutes mushrooms' natural flavor.

PENNE PASTA WITH BLUE CHEESE AND WALNUTS

This is a rich-tasting but fairly light pasta dish, because it lets the cheese make its own sauce. With any interesting sauce, we like to use tube pasta, such as penne or ziti, which lets the sauce get inside. A ridged pasta such as rigatoni holds sauce well but might be too big and chewy for this subtle sauce. Honestly, in a pinch any pasta will do.

For the blue cheese, your best choices are Danish blue, Maytag blue, Roquefort, or Gorgonzola. If you use either of the latter two, make sure they're young and firm, since they get stronger as they age, and heating makes flavors stronger still; you don't want this dish to be overwhelmingly pungent.

To make this pasta go further, or if you're feeding an especially hungry crowd, you can sauté some spinach and/or chicken in a little garlicky oil and toss it in at the end.

8 ounces penne pasta
2 tablespoons olive oil, plus extra for the pasta
12 ounces crumbled blue cheese
½ cup chopped walnuts
1 tablespoon chopped fresh basil

1. Cook the pasta according to the package directions. Drain and toss with a little olive oil to keep it from sticking together, and cover to keep warm.

2. Heat the 2 tablespoons olive oil in a large skillet over medium heat and add the cheese. Stir constantly until the cheese is melted. Pour the melted cheese over the pasta, sprinkle with the walnuts and basil, and toss well. Serve immediately.

SAUSAGED-AND-PEPPERED PASTA

Pasta served with sausage and peppers is traditional Italian fare. We've lightened it up by making the flavors into a fresh sauce that goes well with any pasta, particularly a tubular or ridged pasta that catches the sauce in every bite.

4 ¢ SERVINGS

- 8   ounces penne, ziti, or other pasta
- 3   tablespoons olive oil, plus extra for the pasta
- ¾   pound hot or sweet Italian sausages (2 or 3 sausages)
- 1   green bell pepper, seeded and chopped
- 2   tablespoons chopped onion (preferably a sweet onion such as Vidalia)
- 1½ teaspoons minced garlic
- 2   pounds tomatoes, seeded and chopped, or one 28-ounce can diced tomatoes, drained
- 1   tablespoon lemon juice
- 1   teaspoon dried Italian seasoning

1. Cook the pasta according to the package directions. Drain and toss with a little olive oil to keep it from sticking together, and cover to keep warm. Set aside.

2. Fill a large skillet halfway with water. Prick the sausages with a fork, add them to the water in the skillet, turn the heat up to high, and bring to a boil. Lower the heat to medium-high and boil for 5 minutes. (The sausages do not need to be fully cooked at this point). Drain. Rinse the sausages under cold water. Run a sharp knife down the length of each sausage and peel off the casing. Using a serrated knife, cut the sausages into ½-inch-thick slices.

3. Wipe the skillet clean and add 2 tablespoons of the oil. Set over medium-high heat and heat the oil until it shimmers. Add the bell pepper, onion, and garlic and cook, stirring, to flavor the oil, for about 2 minutes. Stir in the tomatoes and the sliced sausage. Reduce the heat to medium and cook, stirring frequently, until the sausages are cooked and the bell pepper is tender, 6 to 8 minutes.

4. Meanwhile, in a small bowl combine the remaining 1 tablespoon oil with the lemon juice and Italian seasoning. Stir the mixture into the hot drained pasta.

5. In a large serving bowl, combine the pasta with the sausage mixture, toss, and serve immediately.

ASIAN-STYLE NUTTY NOODLES

This is a relatively light and sophisticated dish that gets its protein from nuts, but kids usually love it just because they can't get over the fact that you're cooking with peanut butter! Asian egg noodles are also called Chinese egg noodles, mein, or somen; most Asian noodles found in supermarkets are not made with egg, so if you can't find them, it's perfectly fine to substitute linguine. Dark sesame oil helps give this some added flavor, but if you can't find it you can substitute peanut oil.

4 SERVINGS ¢

12 ounces Asian egg noodles
⅓ cup sesame seeds
¼ cup smooth peanut butter
2 tablespoons soy sauce (preferably low sodium)
1 teaspoon sesame oil
1 teaspoon minced garlic
1 teaspoon red pepper flakes
1 medium cucumber, peeled, seeded, and chopped
1 scallion, thinly sliced (green part only)

1. Cook the noodles according to the package directions. Rinse well, drain, put the noodles in a large bowl, cover to keep warm, and set aside.
2. While the noodles are cooking, toast the sesame seeds in a dry skillet over medium heat, stirring frequently, until golden, about 5 minutes.
3. Melt the peanut butter in the microwave or in the top of a double boiler until it's soft and runny. With an electric mixer or in a blender, combine the peanut butter with the soy sauce, oil, garlic, and red pepper flakes. If the mixture is too thick, add very hot water a tablespoon at a time until it reaches a pouring consistency. Pour over the noodles and toss to coat.
4. Sprinkle the toasted sesame seeds on top of the noodles and garnish with the cucumber and scallion.

ROTINI WITH ASPARAGUS AND PROSCIUTTO

This is a pretty dish that uses some sophisticated, and sometimes pricey, ingredients, but in small enough quantities to be affordable. If asparagus is out of season, you can substitute leeks (white parts only) or broccoli (stems and florets). Prosciutto is a delicately salty Italian ham that can be replaced with Serrano ham, Parma ham, Black Forest ham, or lean bacon that you've boiled for a couple of minutes, then rinsed and dried.

We love the way the rotini (spiral pasta) looks alongside the straight asparagus, but this is visually interesting with small shell pasta or farfalle (bow-tie pasta), too.

4 SERVINGS $

8   ounces rotini pasta
    Olive oil
½   pound asparagus, trimmed
    and cut into 1-inch
    segments
¼   pound thinly sliced
    prosciutto, cut crosswise
    into ½-inch pieces
1   cup half-and-half
⅛   teaspoon ground nutmeg
⅓   cup grated Parmesan
    cheese
    Salt and freshly ground
    black pepper

1. Cook the pasta according to the package directions, adding a bit of oil to the water to keep the pasta from sticking together. Add the asparagus during the last 5 minutes of cooking. Drain, pour into a large serving bowl, and set aside.

2. Meanwhile, add the prosciutto to a large skillet over medium heat, stirring a little to heat (but not cook) the prosciutto, for 1 to 2 minutes. Add the half-and-half and nutmeg, bring to a boil, and continue to boil, stirring, for 1 minute. Pour over the pasta.

3. Sprinkle the pasta with the Parmesan, plus salt and pepper to taste. Toss well and serve immediately.

TIPS > Did you make too much pasta? Don't throw it away. Toss it with a little bit of olive oil and store in the refrigerator, tightly covered. The next day, heat a cup of pasta sauce in a frying pan, and when it's simmering, little by little add the leftover pasta until it's heated through. Or chop the leftover pasta up and add it to soup just before serving.

LINGUINE IN SMOKIN' CLAM SAUCE

Pasta in red or white clam sauce is a staple of many a cook, but my friend Lisa Vernon gives this a twist by using smoked clams.

SERVINGS

8   ounces linguine
     Olive oil
2   6.5-ounce cans smoked
     clams in oil
1½   teaspoons minced garlic
1   14-ounce can plum
     tomatoes, undrained
1   cup tomato sauce
     Salt and freshly ground
     black pepper
2   tablespoons grated
     Parmesan cheese
2   tablespoons chopped fresh
     parsley
1   small lemon, cut into
     wedges

1. Cook the pasta according to the package directions. Drain and toss with a little olive oil to keep it from sticking together and cover to keep warm. Set aside.

2. Pour the oil from the clams into a large skillet over medium heat. Add the garlic and cook, stirring, until fragrant but not browned, 2 to 3 minutes. Stir in the smoked clams. Pour the juice from the canned tomatoes into the skillet and stir. Coarsely chop the tomatoes and add them to the skillet. Stir in the tomato sauce. Cover and simmer for 10 minutes, stirring occasionally to make sure nothing sticks to the bottom. Add salt and pepper to taste.

3. Arrange the cooked linguine on a serving platter. Pour the clam mixture over the top. Sprinkle with the Parmesan and parsley. Squeeze the juice of one lemon wedge over the dish, and garnish with the remaining wedges. Serve immediately.

CHICKEN "ALFREDO" PRIMAVERA WITH WHOLE WHEAT PASTA

Alfredo sauce is yummy, but it's usually made with cream and eggs. I combined our lower-fat version of a yummy cream sauce with a recipe for pasta primavera (lots of veggies) and added chicken and whole wheat pasta for a really healthy meal. Cooking with fresh vegetables is always best, but both spinach and peas are good frozen alternatives—in fact, frozen peas can be more reliably sweet than fresh ones.

4 $ SERVINGS

12 ounces whole wheat linguine
10 ounces frozen chopped spinach
6 to 8 ounces green beans, sliced into 1-inch lengths (about 1 cup sliced)
1 cup frozen peas
3 tablespoons butter or margarine
2 tablespoons all-purpose flour
2 cups skim milk
¼ teaspoon salt
Freshly ground black pepper
16 ounces shredded low-fat Swiss cheese (2 cups)
2 cups diced cooked chicken
¼ cup chopped fresh basil

1. Cook the linguine according to the package directions, adding the spinach, the green beans, and the peas to the cooking water during the last 5 minutes of cooking. Drain and return the pasta and vegetables to the pot.

2. While the linguine is cooking, melt the butter in a medium-size saucepan over medium heat. Sprinkle the flour over the melted butter and cook, stirring constantly, for 1 minute. Gradually add the milk and bring to a simmer, stirring frequently. Stir in the salt and a couple of grindings of pepper. Add the cheese slowly, stirring until it melts.

3. Return the pot of cooked pasta and vegetables to low heat. Add the cheese sauce and the chicken and mix well. Transfer to serving plates and garnish with the chopped basil. Serve immediately.

FABULOUS

FISH

"After experiments with many different ways of preparing and seasoning fish, broiled fish with my Cajun seasoning has become one of my son's favorite meals."

Fish is quick and easy to prepare, not to mention a healthy food to enjoy several times a week. Some fish is expensive, it's true, but smart shopping will usually turn

up one or more affordable varieties. Frozen fish from other countries is also often reasonable, and it tastes fine when cooked in liquid or with spices or sauces.

Many people who are not accustomed to eating fish believe that all varieties have a strong fishy odor and flavor. This is a myth. Many fish, such as tilapia, halibut, catfish, and haddock, have a very mild flavor. In fact, when fish is fresh, it should have very little odor at all.

Any strong fishy odor emanating from fish is usually a good indication that the fish has been sitting around too long.

Like a lot of kids, when my son asks what's for dinner, "fish" is not typically the answer he's hoping to hear. But I make a Cajun seasoning for fish that gives it a good kick and takes my mind to the bayous of Louisiana. After experiments with many different ways of preparing and seasoning fish, broiled

fish with my Cajun seasoning has become one of my son's favorite meals.

Always remember to rinse fish well under cold running water and pat it dry with a paper towel before cooking. Do not soak fish in water, as doing so tends to break down its flavor. And remember, fish cooks quickly, so keep an eye on it and do not overcook! Fish that is properly cooked should flake easily with a fork but still have some resistance.

CAJUN JUMPING FISH STEW

Catfish are common in the bayou, so all sorts of interesting and reasonable fish dishes are part of Louisiana cuisine. This hearty fish stew "jumps" thanks to some spicy red pepper.

4 SERVINGS $

- 2 tablespoons olive oil
- 1 onion, minced
- 1 cup chopped celery
- 2 teaspoons minced garlic
- 2 10.5-ounce cans vegetable broth
- 1 6-ounce can tomato paste
- 1 pound catfish fillets
- 1 tablespoon lemon juice
- 1 teaspoon red pepper flakes (optional)
- 2 cups hot cooked white rice
- ¼ cup chopped fresh parsley

1. Heat the oil in a large skillet over medium-high heat until it shimmers. Add the onion, celery, and garlic and cook, stirring, until softened, 2 to 3 minutes. Add the vegetable broth and tomato paste, stir until well blended, and bring to a boil.

2. Add the catfish to the skillet and reduce the heat to medium. Add the lemon juice and at least a few red pepper flakes (use the full teaspoon if you like things spicy). Cover and simmer until the catfish flakes with a fork, 10 minutes or more depending on thickness.

3. Put the hot rice on a platter. With a spatula, remove the fish from the skillet and put it on top of the rice. Raise the heat under the skillet to medium-high and bring the remaining liquid to a boil, scraping the bottom of the pan and stirring until the sauce is well blended. Ladle the sauce over the fish and rice and garnish with the parsley.

TIPS > + +

Always remember to rinse fish well under cold running water and pat it dry with a paper towel before cooking.

COCONUT SNAPPER WITH COLORFUL RICE

Red snapper is a flavorful, meaty fish that stands up well to other flavors. If you have nice fresh snapper, it's almost a shame to cook it in a sauce; save this recipe for snapper you've bought on sale and frozen (and, of course, thawed before cooking). This can be made equally well with tilapia, which is usually inexpensive, especially the frozen kind.

SERVINGS

4 red snapper fillets (4 to 6 ounces each)
1 teaspoon garlic powder
  Salt and freshly ground black pepper
1 lemon, halved
4 tablespoons olive oil
1 red onion, chopped
4 plum tomatoes, diced
1 yellow bell pepper, seeded and chopped
1 green bell pepper, seeded and chopped
2 teaspoons minced fresh ginger
¼ cup chopped fresh parsley
1 tablespoon tomato paste
1 cup coconut milk
  All-purpose flour
2 cups hot cooked white or yellow rice

1. Sprinkle the fish with the garlic powder, some salt and pepper, and the juice of ½ lemon. Cover and let sit while you prepare the rest of the dish.

2. Add 2 tablespoons of the oil to a skillet over medium heat. Add 1 tablespoon each of the onion, tomatoes, and yellow and green peppers along with ½ teaspoon of the ginger and cook, stirring frequently, for about 2 minutes. Remove the cooked vegetables with a slotted spoon to a small bowl and set aside.

3. Add the remaining vegetables and ginger to the skillet and cook, stirring frequently, until the vegetables are tender, 8 to 10 minutes. Add the parsley, tomato paste, and 1 cup water to the pan. Raise the heat to medium-high, and when the liquid begins to bubble, reduce the heat and simmer until it has formed a well-blended sauce, about 5 minutes. Pour in the coconut milk and stir well. Turn off the heat.

4. Dust the fish fillets with flour. Add the remaining 2 tablespoons oil to a large skillet over medium-high heat and heat until the oil pops when you sprinkle water on it. Lower the heat to medium and panfry the fish until golden, about 3 minutes on each side. Spoon off any excess oil from the pan, and add the sauce to the fish in the skillet. Lower the heat and simmer until the fish is flaky, about 10 minutes.

5. Stir the reserved chopped vegetables into the rice. Cut the remaining ½ lemon into wedges for garnish. Serve the fish over the rice, spooning the sauce over all.

LAID-BACK CREOLE CATFISH WITH OKRA

SERVINGS

Catfish is one of the most affordable fish you can buy at the market, and it is also plentiful in the bayou, which is why it features prominently in Creole and Cajun cuisine. If you already have some pike or whitefish handy, those can be substituted for catfish in most recipes.

Some people find okra an acquired taste. It serves double duty as a thickener, so if you really want to substitute for the okra (asparagus or eggplant will work, as long as you microwave them for a few minutes first, since they take longer to cook than okra), you will also need to add ⅓ tablespoon gumbo filé powder at the very end of the cooking process or your sauce will be too runny.

Creole seasoning and chili powder can be acquired tastes too, so we suggest you start with ¼ teaspoon of each and adjust to taste later.

4 catfish fillets (¾ to 1 pound total)
¼ teaspoon Creole seasoning
1 15.5-ounce can black-eyed peas, rinsed and drained
1 cup sliced okra
1 8-ounce can tomato sauce
2 large carrots, peeled and sliced about ¼ inch thick
1 medium onion, sliced about ¼ inch thick
1½ teaspoons minced garlic
1 teaspoon chili powder
½ teaspoon dried oregano
2 cups hot cooked white rice

1. Preheat the oven to 350°F.
2. Season the fish with the Creole seasoning. Place them in a lightly greased 9 x 13-inch baking dish and bake for 15 to 20 minutes, until the fish flakes easily with a fork.
3. While the fish is baking, place a large skillet over medium-high heat. Add the black-eyed peas, okra, tomato sauce, carrots, onion, garlic, chili powder, and oregano, and bring to a boil. Reduce the heat to medium and simmer, covered, until the carrots are tender, about 20 minutes.
4. Spoon the vegetable mixture over the rice and serve with the baked catfish.

TIPS > When you buy filleted fish, some small bones, called pin bones, may remain. Keep a large pair of tweezers handy to remove them before cooking. Squeeze the fish with your fingers to find them.

FRUGAL FISH TACOS

It can be less expensive to buy some ready-made ingredients than to make them yourself; salsa verde is a case in point. Unless you want to make it up in large quantities from tomatillos, garlic, cilantro, jalapeño chiles, onions, and lime juice, just buy some to keep on hand. You can doctor it—in this case, we add mango—to make it your own or to pair it with different dishes; that makes it go further, too.

Similarly, mojo sauce is available bottled; I favor the Cuban version. If you get "mojomania" and want to make it yourself, it's pretty simple: Mash 3 cloves garlic and blend with ¼ cup olive oil, 2 tablespoons chopped onion, 2 teaspoons salt, ⅛ teaspoon dried oregano, and a pinch of cumin. Then add the juice of 3 sour oranges (or the juice of 1 sweet orange plus the juice of 2 lemons and 3 limes). Run it all through a blender to form the sauce.

Several brands of yellow rice–and–black beans are available, making an easy all-in-one side dish to go with these tacos devised by my friend Rachael Johnson.

1 **pound inexpensive white fish (catfish, tilapia, etc.)**
Salt and freshly ground black pepper
1 **cup mojo sauce (see headnote)**
1 **cup salsa verde**
1 **mango, peeled and diced**
1 **cup cooked corn kernels (fresh, or canned and drained)**
¼ **cup lime juice**
¼ **cup lemon juice**
Four 10-inch whole wheat tortillas
¼ **cup olive oil**
Lettuce
1 **package yellow rice with black beans, cooked according to the package directions**
Slices of lemon and lime for garnish (optional)

1. Preheat the oven to 350°F.
2. Place the fish in a shallow pan and sprinkle it lightly with a little salt and pepper. Pour the mojo sauce over the fish and let sit to marinate for at least 30 minutes and no longer than an hour. (Marinating longer will actually cook the fish, so be careful.)
3. While the fish is marinating, combine the salsa verde, mango, corn, lime juice, and lemon juice in a medium-size bowl. Cover and set aside to let the flavors blend.
4. Wrap the tortillas in aluminum foil and place in the oven for 5 to 7 minutes, or until warm.
5. When the fish is finished marinating, heat the oil in a large skillet over medium-high heat. Add the fish, discarding the marinade, and brown it lightly on each side. Lower the temperature to medium-low and cook until the fish begins to flake when poked with a fork, 3 to 5 minutes.
6. Place the tortillas on individual plates or on a serving platter and cover each with torn pieces of lettuce. Divide the fish equally and put it on top of the lettuce. Roll up the wraps tightly, securing if necessary with toothpicks. Serve with the rice and beans and the salsa as side dishes. Garnish the tacos with lemon and lime slices, if desired.

LEMON-LIME VEGGIE TILAPIA

Tilapia is one of the most affordable of the lean, firm fish. You can substitute bass, orange roughy, or flounder in this recipe.

SERVINGS

Fish is quick and easy to prepare, not to mention a healthy food to enjoy several times a week.

8	ounces linguine
1	tablespoon plus 1 teaspoon olive oil, plus extra for the pasta
4	tilapia fillets (about 1 pound total)
1	tablespoon lemon juice
¼	teaspoon garlic salt
¼	teaspoon freshly ground black pepper
¼	teaspoon dried oregano
⅛	teaspoon paprika
1	zucchini, sliced ¼ inch thick
¼	cup corn kernels
½	red bell pepper, chopped
1	tablespoon lime juice
1	teaspoon minced garlic
3	to 4 drops hot sauce

1. Preheat the oven to 375°F.

2. Cook the pasta according to the package directions. Drain, toss with a little oil to keep it from sticking, cover to keep warm, and set aside.

3. Meanwhile, place the fish in a lightly oiled 9 x 13 inch baking pan. In a small mixing bowl, blend the 1 tablespoon oil, the lemon juice, garlic salt, black pepper, and oregano, and pour the mixture evenly over the fish. Sprinkle the paprika over the top.

4. In a medium-size mixing bowl, combine the zucchini, corn, bell pepper, lime juice, garlic, the remaining 1 teaspoon oil, and the hot sauce, then pour the vegetable mixture into an 8 x 8-inch square baking dish.

5. Bake the dishes of fish and vegetables side by side for about 20 minutes, or until the vegetables are tender and the fish flakes easily with a fork.

6. Serve the fish over the pasta, surrounded by the vegetables.

SMOTHERED CATFISH WITH ZESTY GREEN BEANS AND PASTA

SERVINGS

A tasty crust "smothers" this catfish, so we balance it by giving the green beans a little "oomph" of their own; that way they don't just fade into the background. If catfish isn't handy, you can use another firm, fat fish such as perch or whitefish, or a slightly leaner fish such as grouper or mahi mahi. And if you can't find peach marmalade, never fear— any flavor of marmalade will do.

8   ounces spaghetti or linguine
2   teaspoons olive oil, plus extra for the pasta
4   catfish fillets (1 to 1½ pounds total)
    Salt and freshly ground black pepper
2   tablespoons peach marmalade
1   tablespoon low-fat smooth peanut butter
1½ teaspoons minced garlic
½   teaspoon paprika
¼   teaspoon cayenne pepper
¼   cup dry-roasted peanuts, chopped
¾   pound green beans, ends trimmed
½   tablespoon lemon juice

1. Preheat the oven to 450°F.

2. Cook the pasta according to the package directions. Drain, toss with a little olive oil to keep from sticking, cover, and set aside.

3. Meanwhile, place the catfish in a lightly oiled 9 x 13-inch baking dish. Drizzle with 1 teaspoon of the olive oil and sprinkle with a little salt and black pepper.

4. In a small mixing bowl, combine the marmalade, peanut butter, ½ teaspoon of the garlic, the paprika, and cayenne. Stir in the peanuts. Spread the mixture evenly over the fish fillets. Bake until the fish flakes easily with a fork, about 10 minutes depending on thickness.

5. While the fish is cooking, put the green beans on a microwave-safe plate. Drizzle with the remaining 1 teaspoon olive oil. Sprinkle with the lemon juice, the remaining 1 teaspoon garlic, and one or two gratings of black pepper. Microwave on high, loosely covered, until the beans are crisp-tender, 3 to 5 minutes.

6. Use a spatula to transfer the catfish to individual plates or a platter with the cooked pasta. Serve the beans on the side.

TIPS >
When you buy filleted fish, some small bones, called pin bones, may remain. Keep a large pair of tweezers handy to remove them before cooking. Squeeze the fish with your fingers to find them.

THE CHAMP'S BAKED SALMON WITH WILD RICE AND MUSHROOMS

World light-heavyweight boxing champ Antonio Tarver cares a lot about healthy eating. He says that his mom and sisters did all the cooking at home when he was growing up, but that he's made up for lost time with simple, healthy meals that don't take much time to make; this is his favorite. Wild rice can be expensive, but it's easy to find packaged long grain-and-wild rice mixes that would make an excellent substitute.

2 SERVINGS **$**

1   tablespoon slivered almonds
2   salmon steaks, each ¾ inch thick (6 to 8 ounces each)
     Salt and freshly ground black pepper
1   cup dry white wine or cooking sherry
1   tablespoon butter, melted
2   teaspoons lemon juice
1   teaspoon minced garlic
½   to ⅔ cup wild rice
2   cups sliced mushrooms
¼   cup chopped onion
1   teaspoon butter
2   sprigs fresh rosemary (optional)

1. Preheat the oven to 350°F.
2. In a small nonstick skillet over medium-low heat, toast the almonds, shaking the skillet often to prevent the almonds from burning, for 2 to 3 minutes.
3. Sprinkle both sides of each salmon steak very lightly with salt and pepper, and put into a lightly oiled 8 x 8-inch square baking dish. Pour the wine over the top. In a small mixing bowl, combine the melted butter, lemon juice, and garlic. Pour over the salmon. Bake for 35 minutes, or until the salmon flakes when prodded with a fork.
4. Meanwhile, begin to cook the rice according to the package directions. When the rice has come to a boil, stir in the mushrooms, onion, and butter. Cook over low heat, covered, for as long as the package says to cook the rice, usually 20 to 30 minutes.
5. Stir the toasted almonds into the rice and serve on individual plates. Place a salmon steak on each plate and garnish with a sprig of rosemary, if desired.

PECAN-CRUSTED TILAPIA WITH MANGO-SALSA SALAD AND COCONUT RICE

This recipe is equally good with any lean, firm fish such as bass or flounder, and the flavorful pecan coating adds a bit of oomph to previously frozen fish. A fruit salsa is a great accompaniment to any simple fish, but here we turned our salsa ingredients into a salad. The Caribbean flair of the mango is partnered with coconut rice, but plain white rice or pasta could also be used.

4 SERVINGS **$**

4   tilapia fillets (about 1 pound total)
2   large egg whites, beaten
1½ cups pecans, finely chopped or processed in a food processor
2   cups coconut milk
1   cup jasmine rice
1   cup diced tomatoes
½   medium red onion, finely chopped
1   jalapeño chile, minced
1½ tablespoons chopped fresh cilantro leaves
    Juice of 2 limes
1   tablespoon olive oil
    Salt and freshly ground black pepper
2   cups mixed salad greens
1   large ripe mango, peeled, pitted, and sliced

1. Preheat the oven to 350°F.
2. Dip each piece of fish in the egg whites, then in the chopped pecans to coat both sides well. Place the fish in a lightly oiled 9 x 13-inch baking dish. Bake for 18 to 20 minutes, or until the fish is opaque and flakes easily with a fork.
3. Bring the coconut milk and ½ cup water to a boil in a medium-size pot over high heat. Stir in the rice and mix well. Reduce the heat to low, cover, and cook for 15 minutes. Remove from the heat and let sit for about 5 minutes. Fluff with a fork before serving.

4. While the fish and the rice are cooking, combine the tomatoes, onion, jalapeño, and cilantro in a bowl. Add the lime juice and oil and stir well to blend. Season to taste with salt and pepper.
5. Divide the salad greens among four plates. Evenly divide the mango slices among the four plates of greens and top each with one-quarter of the tomato salsa dressing.
6. Carefully transfer the fish with a spatula to individual plates or a serving platter and serve with the rice, with the salad on the side.

BAKED COD WITH AVOCADO-CORN SALSA

As you can probably tell by now, I'm a big fan of homemade salsas; they're a great alternative to vegetables and salads and are a terrific accompaniment to a simple—and fast—baked fish. This cod recipe can be made equally well with haddock, pollock, flounder, or sole.

SERVINGS $

2 large avocados, pitted and diced
1 14-ounce can corn kernels, drained
2 large tomatoes, seeded and diced
2 tablespoons chopped fresh parsley
1 small lime
4 cod fillets (1 to 1½ pounds total)
1 tablespoon plus 1 teaspoon olive oil
   Salt and freshly ground black pepper
1 15-ounce can whole white potatoes, drained
1 tablespoon onion flakes

1. Preheat the oven to 350°F.
2. In a medium-size mixing bowl, combine the avocado, corn, tomatoes, parsley, and juice of ½ lime. Chill until ready to serve.
3. Place the cod fillets in a lightly oiled 9 x 13-inch baking dish. Drizzle with 1 teaspoon of the oil and the juice of the remaining ½ lime; sprinkle with salt and pepper. Bake for about 20 minutes, or until the fish flakes easily with a fork.

4. While the fish is baking, add the remaining 1 tablespoon oil to a medium-size skillet over medium-high heat. Rinse and dry the canned potatoes and add them to the hot oil, stirring. Sprinkle the onion flakes over the potatoes. Cook, stirring, until the potatoes are brown on all sides, 1 to 2 minutes.
5. Serve the fish hot, topped by the cold salsa, with the potatoes on the side.

FISH IN WHITE WINE

One day I was looking for something to do with one of those boxes of anonymous frozen fish fillets—you know, the ones that look like a brick once the box is peeled away. They're hard to thaw in the microwave because the outside of the "brick" starts to cook while the inside stays rock hard. Aha, I thought, let's poach it. Believe it or not, this has now turned into a favorite fast fish meal. Use any mild fish, such as cod, scrod, haddock, sole, or tilapia.

- 3½ **tablespoons butter**
- ½ **cup sliced button mushrooms**
- 1 **tablespoon chopped onion**
- 1 **¾-pound package frozen mild fish fillets, at least partially thawed**
- ½ **cup dry white wine Salt**
- 1½ **tablespoons all-purpose flour**
- 2 **tablespoons light cream or milk**
- 1 **cup hot cooked white rice**

1. Melt 2 tablespoons of the butter in a 10-inch skillet over medium-low heat. Scatter the mushrooms and onion across the bottom of the pan.

2. Peel off the individual fillets of fish from the block. If the center is still frozen, add it to the pan. Pour the wine over the fish and bring it to a boil over moderate heat. (Peel off any frozen fish fillets as they thaw.) Sprinkle the fillets lightly with salt and arrange side-by-side in the skillet.

3. Reduce the heat to medium-low and cook the fish until it flakes easily, about 10 minutes. Remove the fish with a spatula to a plate. Pour off the fish liquid into a measuring cup,

adding water if necessary to make ⅓ cup.

4. Add the remaining 1½ tablespoons butter to the skillet and melt over medium-low heat. Gradually add the flour, stirring constantly, and cook until the mixture bubbles. Gradually add back the fish liquid, whisking until the sauce is thoroughly blended. Stir in the cream and cook until the sauce is smooth and hot, 2 to 4 minutes. Scrape the bottom of the pan with a spatula to incorporate any last bits of onion, mushroom, and fish.

5. Pour the sauce over the fish to serve. Serve with the rice.

TIPS >
Instead of discarding leftover wine, freeze it in a plastic tub (filled no more than two-thirds full, since it will expand as it freezes) or ice-cube tray. Then you can use the frozen wine in recipes that call for wine without having to open a bottle.

SENSATIONAL
SEAFOOD

"Frozen seafood, especially shrimp, makes a great staple to keep on hand."

Like fish, seafood cooks fast, which makes it great for a last-minute meal. Too many people think of seafood as something expensive and elaborate to save for special

occasions. Instead of thinking lobster and oysters, think shrimp, clams, mussels, and scallops, and you'll broaden your kitchen repertoire without busting your budget.

Frozen seafood, especially shrimp, makes a great staple to keep on hand. There are so many easy dishes you can make with shrimp that my family stocks up whenever we see large bags of frozen shrimp on sale. While most kinds of seafood lose flavor once frozen, cook them in a nice sauce and you won't notice the difference. And if you like crabmeat, remember to try surimi, better known as imitation crabmeat, crab sticks, or "sea legs"; it's made from fish and is both less expensive than crab and hypoallergenic for people with seafood allergies (of whom, unfortunately, I am one).

SUNNY SHRIMP CURRY

This is a really easy, tasty curry. It's perfectly good made with frozen shrimp. For most recipes, the size of the shrimp you choose is a personal preference, and it can also be dictated by price. Shrimp sizes are generally referenced by "count"—that is, how many shrimp to a pound, which is a general indicator of size. Instead, use about ¼ pound per person and pick the size that's priced best by the pound. Shrimp in the shell is usually less expensive, and the shells only count for about 10 percent of the weight. Depending on the recipe, you can leave the shells on, or take them off before cooking; when there's a sauce, we like to remove the shells first, because it's easiest to do with your fingers! Serve with your favorite rice; I like it with jasmine rice, myself.

2   tablespoons canola oil
1   large onion, chopped
1   tablespoon curry powder
1   10.5-ounce can low-sodium chicken broth
    Freshly ground black pepper
1   to 1½ pounds large shrimp, shelled and deveined
1   10.5-ounce box frozen peas
    Salt (optional)
2   tablespoons all-purpose flour
1   tablespoon grated fresh ginger
    Juice of 1 lime
2   large tomatoes
½   cup shredded unsweetened coconut

1. Heat the oil in a large skillet over medium heat. Add the onion and cook, stirring, until softened, about 5 minutes. Stir in the curry powder and cook for 1 minute, stirring constantly. Add the broth and a dash or two of pepper, then add the shrimp and peas. Bring to a boil, then reduce the heat and simmer for 5 minutes. Add salt to taste, if desired.

2. While the shrimp is cooking, add the flour, ginger, and lime juice to a small mixing bowl and stir until blended. You can add a splash of water if the flour mixture gets too thick to stir. Pour the contents of the bowl into the skillet with the shrimp and cook, stirring, until the sauce thickens, about 1 minute. Cut the tomatoes into wedges, cut each wedge in half, and add to the skillet. Cover and simmer for about 5 more minutes.

3. To serve, garnish with the shredded coconut.

SHRIMP SCAMPI

Scampi is another really simple dish that somehow has a reputation as gourmet fare; we won't tell anyone how easy it is if you don't! Serve over pasta al dente with a simple green salad and, if you like, some crusty Italian bread.

SERVINGS

¾ **pound medium shrimp, shelled and deveined**
4 **tablespoons butter**
2 **tablespoons olive oil**
¼ **cup minced garlic**
¼ **cup dry white wine or vegetable broth**
  Juice of 1 small lemon
2 **tablespoons chopped fresh parsley**
  Salt and freshly ground black pepper
8 **ounces linguine, cooked according to the package directions and kept warm**

1. Rinse the shrimp and pat dry with paper towels.
2. Heat the butter in a large skillet over medium heat. Add the oil and continue to heat. Add the garlic and cook, stirring, until softened but not browned, 1 to 2 minutes. Add the shrimp, wine, and lemon juice. Cook, stirring and tossing carefully, until the shrimp are bright pink, about 2 minutes; do not overcook. Add the parsley and season with salt and pepper to taste.
3. Put the pasta in a bowl, pour the shrimp—pan juices and all—over the top, and toss well.

SOUTHERN STYLE SHRIMP ÉTOUFFÉE

Crawfish étouffée is a traditional New Orleans dish that can be made with more readily available shrimp. The key to a good étouffée is the roux; although it's simply flour cooked in butter, it can take some practice to get it nice and dark without burning it.

4 SERVINGS $

4 tablespoons butter
3 tablespoons all-purpose flour
1 cup chopped sweet onion
⅓ cup shelled sweet baby peas
1 red bell pepper, seeded and chopped
2 tablespoons chopped fresh parsley
½ teaspoon minced garlic
1 pound medium shrimp, peeled and deveined
  Juice of ½ lime
2 to 3 drops hot sauce
  Salt and freshly ground black pepper
2 cups hot cooked white rice

1. Melt the butter in a large skillet over medium heat until it is liquid. Gradually whisk in the flour and cook, stirring continuously, until the flour turns a deep golden brown but does not overcook or burn, about 15 to 30 minutes.

2. Stir in ½ cup warm water until blended. Add the onion, peas, bell pepper, parsley, and garlic and cook, stirring occasionally, for 5 minutes. Stir in the shrimp and cook until the shrimp is bright pink and firm and the bell pepper is tender, about 5 minutes more. Stir in the lime juice and hot sauce. Add salt and black pepper to taste.

3. Pour the contents of the pan over the rice to serve.

SEAFOOD BISQUE

I generally try to avoid canned soups for cooking or serving at dinnertime, but I don't mind doctoring them when it comes to fish and seafood, because fish stock is time-consuming to make and hard to find in stores. This recipe starts with canned clam chowder, but you'd never recognize it as anything other than homemade by the time you're done! To keep the cost down, we use surimi—most commonly called "sea legs" or imitation crabmeat. It's made from fresh fish that's been pounded, flavored, and re-formed into crab-leg shapes. For a main course, serve with a tossed salad.

4 SERVINGS $

1   10.5-ounce can New England–style clam chowder
4   sea scallops or 16 bay scallops
1   12-ounce can baby potatoes, drained
½   pound crab substitute
1   cup heavy cream
1   handful fresh spinach
    Splash of dry white wine or sherry
¼   teaspoon minced fresh dill (or ⅛ teaspoon dried)
    Salt and freshly ground black pepper

1. . Pour the can of clam chowder into a large saucepan; if using condensed, add water according to the package directions. Add the scallops.

2. Cube the potatoes and cut the crab substitute into chunks. Add the potatoes and crab substitute to the soup, along with the cream, spinach, wine, dill, and salt and pepper to taste, and stir to combine. Bring to a simmer over medium heat, then reduce the heat to low and simmer for 5 minutes. Serve in bowls.

TIPS >

Fresh herbs are preferable to use in most recipes, but if a recipe calls for only a small amount, buying a whole bunch can be expensive. Instead of sticking to dried herbs, there are several ways to keep fresh herbs for later use. You can chop the herbs with a little olive oil and store them refrigerated in an airtight jar for up to a week. Or you can make herb butter by working 1 teaspoon of chopped herbs into 1 tablespoon of softened butter; form into a ball, wrap in plastic wrap, and freeze. Use herb butters to cook with, or as a nice topping for beef or chicken.

E-Z Sesame-Ginger Chicken Salad, page 141

Mediterranean Chickpea-Pasta Salad, page 136, Tarragon Chicken Baguettes, page 176

Cheesy Tomato Panini, page 178, Wild West Chili Soup, page 164

Ratatouille with Couscous, page 151, Bok Choy–Shiitake Japanese Stir-Fry, page 156

Pizza Frittata, page 127, Caribbean Lime Chicken with Grilled Pineapple, page 16

Papaya-Mango Chicken, page 21, Steak Fajitas, page 47

Beef Burgundy, page 42, Cranberry Pork with Roasted Red Potatoes, page 53

Finger-Lickin' Pulled Pork with Beans and Corn, page 57, Graham Cracker Fruit Torte, page 193

Cinnamon-Raisin Monkeybread, page 194

SOUTHERN SCALLOPS WITH CORNMEAL AND BOURBON

The American South isn't all "country;" there's plenty of coastline, too, which is why you'll find shellfish in quite a lot of Southern cooking. Here's a real Southern twist to scallops, using cornmeal and bourbon. You can also substitute rounds of a firm-fleshed fish such as cod, shark, or skate for the scallops—a napkin ring makes a good "cookie cutter."

4 SERVINGS $

2½ cups cornmeal
⅓ cup freshly grated Parmesan cheese
3 large eggs
  Salt
2 cups all-purpose flour
16 jumbo sea scallops (1 to 1½ pounds)
4 ounces bourbon
⅓ cup apple cider or apple juice
¼ cup apple cider vinegar
2 shallots, peeled and chopped
2 teaspoons minced garlic
  Juice of ½ lemon
¾ pound (3 sticks) unsalted butter, chilled
  Freshly ground black pepper
2 large green apples, peeled and sliced
  Canola oil for frying
½ pound green beans, ends trimmed and lightly steamed

1. Preheat the broiler.

2. In a small bowl, combine the cornmeal and the Parmesan. In another small bowl, lightly beat the eggs with a dash of salt. Pour the flour onto a dinner plate or pie plate. One at a time, dip the scallops first into the flour, then the eggs, and then the cornmeal mixture. Cover and refrigerate briefly to set the coating.

3. In a saucepan, combine 3 ounces of the bourbon with the cider, vinegar, shallots, and 1 teaspoon of the garlic. Cook over medium heat until almost completely reduced, about 10 minutes. Add the lemon juice and lower the heat. Cut ½ pound (2 sticks) of the chilled butter into small pieces and add to the sauce one by one, stirring gently so that the sauce doesn't separate. Remove from the heat and keep warm; season to taste with salt and pepper.

4. In a small saucepan, melt 6 tablespoons of the remaining butter and stir in the remaining 1 ounce of bourbon. Arrange the apple slices on a nonstick baking sheet and drizzle evenly with the bourbon butter. Broil until the edges of the apples begin to curl, 4 to 5 minutes. Remove from the oven and set aside.

5. Fill a heavy saucepan with oil to a depth of ½ inch. Fry the scallops, in batches if necessary to avoid crowding, until crisp and golden, 2 to 3 minutes per side. Remove with tongs or a slotted spatula, drain on paper towels, and keep warm.

6. Pour off the excess oil and add the remaining 1 teaspoon garlic and the green beans to the saucepan from which you removed the scallops. Cook, stirring, until the green beans are lightly browned and slightly limp, 3 to 5 minutes; they should still have a bit of crunch. Add the remaining 2 tablespoons butter if the pan gets too dry.

7. To serve, divide the apple slices equally among the serving plates. Serve with the scallops on top of the apple slices, with the green beans on the side. Drizzle a little of the bourbon sauce over the scallops and apples; serve the rest on the side.

MARINER'S MUSSELS

Mussels are usually the least expensive shellfish, and they are readily available most of the year. *Moules à la marinière*—mussels in the style of sailors—is a traditional french and Belgian dish and simply means that they are cooked in white wine and herbs. Belgians serve this with french fries, but I like to use lots of crusty bread to sop up every last bit of the delicious garlicky broth. Make sure the mussels you buy have already been scrubbed and debearded (beards are the filaments that mussels use to attach themselves to rocks and docks, and need to be removed if noticeable).

This also makes a great appetizer, in smaller portions.

4 SERVINGS $

2 tablespoons butter
1 tablespoon olive oil
6 to 8 shallots, peeled and chopped
¼ cup minced onion
¼ cup finely chopped fresh parsley
2 teaspoons minced garlic
4 quarts mussels in their shells, scrubbed (4 to 6 pounds)
1½ to 2 cups dry white wine
½ teaspoon salt
2 teaspoons freshly ground black pepper
1 large tomato, chopped and seeded

1. In a large heavy pot over medium heat, melt together the butter and oil. Add the shallots, onion, parsley, and garlic and cook, stirring, until the onions are wilted but not brown, about 2 minutes.
2. Add the mussels, wine, salt, and pepper to the pot, cover tightly, and cook, stirring occasionally, for about 15 minutes. Turn off the heat and stir in the tomato.
3. Ladle into bowls, with plenty of broth, discarding any mussels that didn't open.

JERSEY
JAMBALAYA

I don't know if this recipe is actually from New Jersey, but it's a simplified East Coast version of the New Orleans classic. For the sake of convenience, the frozen green beans with mushrooms are an acceptable substitute for fresh vegetables.

4 $
SERVINGS

1   cup white rice
1   tablespoon canola oil
½   pound shrimp, peeled and deveined
1   medium onion, diced
1   16-ounce can tomatoes, drained
1   9-ounce package frozen green beans with mushrooms
1   teaspoon salt
⅛   teaspoon freshly ground black pepper
⅛   teaspoon dried thyme
2   dashes of Tabasco sauce

1. Cook the rice according to the package directions, but stop the cooking 10 minutes before it's done. Drain and set aside.

2. Heat the oil until it shimmers in a large frying pan over medium-high heat. Add the shrimp and onion and cook, stirring, until the shrimp begins to turn pink. Add the tomatoes, beans with mushrooms, ⅔ cup water, the salt, pepper, thyme, and Tabasco. Bring to a boil, separating the frozen vegetables. Reduce the heat and simmer for 3 minutes.

3. Stir in the partly cooked rice. Cover and simmer for 10 more minutes, until the rice is done.

BILLI-BI
MUSSELS

No one seems to know for sure where the name came from, but one classic billi-bi recipe definitely hails from Brittany. The classic French version is a soup of mussels with saffron and cream in which the mussels are strained out and served separately, but the country version is heartier and more fun. Saffron is one of the most expensive seasonings, but you use such a little bit that it seems to last forever. Muscadet is the only wine native to Brittany, if you want to be authentic, but any white wine, or dry vermouth, will do. Serve with garlic bread and a simple salad.

SERVINGS

4   **tablespoons butter**
6   **tablespoons chopped shallots**
6   **tablespoons chopped onion**
1   **teaspoon minced garlic**
3   **pinches of saffron**
4   **quarts mussels in their shells, scrubbed (4 to 6 pounds)**
2   **cups dry white wine**
½   **cup finely chopped fresh parsley**
     Dash of Tabasco sauce
2   **cups heavy cream**
     Salt and freshly ground black pepper

1. Melt the butter in a deep saucepan or soup pot over medium heat. Add the shallots, onion, garlic, and saffron and cook, stirring, or until the onion is limp and the garlic is a bit fragrant, about 3 minutes.
2. Add the mussels, wine, parsley, and Tabasco. Cover and cook until the mussels pop open, about 5 minutes. Add the cream and bring to a boil. Add salt and pepper to taste.
3. Serve in bowls, discarding any mussels that didn't open

SUPER
SEA
LEGS
SALAD

As we've mentioned, "sea legs" is another name for surimi, a crab substitute made from firm white fish such as pollock. I like it because I'm sensitive to shellfish, but I can eat fish, and this way I can have a seafood salad without being either deprived or itchy. The richness of avocado counters any flavor the substitute might lack.

4 $
SERVINGS

1   **pound crab substitute, flaked**
1   **cup diced celery**
2   **tablespoons diced green bell pepper**
    Juice of 1 lemon
1   **teaspoon salt**
¼   **teaspoon freshly ground black pepper**
4   **to 6 tablespoons mayonnaise**
2   **large ripe avocados, pitted and halved**
    Salad greens

1. In a large bowl, mix together the crab substitute, celery, bell pepper, lemon juice, salt, black pepper, and just enough mayonnaise to hold it together. Adjust the seasonings to taste.

2. Scoop into and over the avocado halves. Garnish each plate with some salad greens.

EXCELLENT
EGGS

"I always keep a dozen eggs in the refrigerator."

From jazzed-up scrambled eggs to elaborate omelets and quiches, with some imagination you can rustle up a last-minute meal anytime there are eggs around.

I always keep a dozen eggs in the refrigerator. Needless to say, eggs make for a pretty inexpensive meal, too.

I don't see anything wrong with having breakfast for dinner once in a while, either. My friend and I both used to get a craving for breakfast at about 9 PM. I recall many times heading to the grocery store at night to grab some eggs and turkey bacon and/or veggie sausage, or pancake mix and all the fixings. I'm sure just about everyone can relate to those cravings. The good thing about having breakfast food

at dinner is that is it can be filling but light—depending on what you cook, of course. Sometimes I'll make an egg white omelet, some turkey bacon for protein, and one pancake for some carbs, and have some juice or fruit for "dessert." It's especially a good thing to do if you don't get around to eating dinner until late, because it's advisable not to eat anything too heavy before you go to bed. When I eat a meal like that, I'm no longer hungry, but when I wake up in the morning I feel great because I ate light.

If your kids are like my son, they

probably love breakfast for dinner, too. It feels like fun. You can bring the kids in on the act; let them make the eggs or whip up the pancake batter. Cooking together brings families together.

Omelets are great at any time of day, but a lot of people are intimidated by making them because the folding-them-over part can be tricky. I offer some recipes in this chapter for different kinds of omelets that don't require special handling.

OPEN BROCCOLI OMELET

Omelets are fair game for dinner, especially when attractively presented. Why hide the ingredients? We serve this omelet open, in pie-shaped slices.

The trick to getting an omelet to cook evenly on top of the stove is to tilt it frequently, lifting the edges a bit so that the liquid can come into contact with the hot pan until the top is no longer runny; then cook just a bit longer to set. Even easier—bake it!

Serve with cubed parsleyed potatoes or, for a lighter meal, sliced fresh fruit.

If you want to be fancy, you can call the potatoes by their French name, *pommes persillade;* a persillade is just a combination of parsley and garlic.

4 ¢ SERVINGS

8   large eggs
¼   teaspoon salt
⅛   teaspoon freshly ground black pepper
1   cup chopped broccoli florets
¼   cup chopped red onion
1   red bell pepper, seeded and chopped
2   tablespoons butter or margarine
4   ounces shredded low-fat Swiss cheese (1 cup)
2   tablespoons olive oil
3   large or 4 medium potatoes, peeled and diced
2   teaspoons chopped fresh parsley
1   teaspoon chopped garlic

1. Preheat the oven to 425°F.
2. In a medium-size bowl, beat together the eggs, ¼ cup water, and the salt and black pepper until blended. Stir in the broccoli, onion, and bell pepper.
3. Melt the butter in a large cast-iron (or other ovenproof) frying pan or a lightly greased 8 x 8-inch square baking pan. Pour in the egg mixture. Sprinkle evenly with the cheese. Bake for about 15 minutes. Reduce the oven temperature to 300°F and bake until a knife inserted in the center comes out clean, 15 to 20 minutes longer. Let stand for 10 minutes before serving.
4. While the omelet is resting, heat the oil in a skillet over medium-high heat. When the oil is hot but not smoking, add the potatoes and cook, turning them frequently, until just lightly browned, about 3 minutes. Add the parsley and garlic and cook, stirring frequently, until the potatoes and garlic are nicely browned, 2 to 3 minutes longer.
5. Slice the open omelet into pie-shaped slices and serve one slice per person, accompanied by the parsleyed potatoes.

HUNGER-STOPPER

The French name for this, *matefaim aux fines herbs*, really just means "hunger-stopper with chopped herbs." It's a cross between an omelet, a pancake, and a soufflé, so it's filling, pretty to look at, and really easy to make. All it needs is a simple salad, and maybe a little warm ham, to make it a complete meal.

Here is a good trick for flipping over a whole omelet: Gently slide it onto a large plate, then carefully place the skillet over the plate and turn everything over to invert it back into the pan so that the uncooked side ends up on the bottom.

4 ¢ SERVINGS

4   **large eggs, separated**
1   **cup sifted all-purpose flour**
¾   **cup milk**
2   **tablespoons chopped fresh parsley**
1   **tablespoon chopped fresh chives**
1   **teaspoon chopped fresh tarragon**
2   **tablespoons butter**
4   **thin slices baked or boiled ham (optional)**

1. In a medium-size bowl, whisk the egg yolks with a fork. Gradually whisk in the flour. While constantly stirring, slowly add the milk until it forms a smooth batter. Lightly stir in the parsley, chives, and tarragon.
2. In another medium-size bowl with an electric mixer or whisk, beat the egg whites until they form stiff peaks. Gently fold them into the yolk mixture so that you no longer see streaks of white, but don't let all the air out of the egg whites.
3. Melt 1 tablespoon of the butter in a 12-inch frying pan over medium heat and tilt the pan so that the bottom is completely covered with the melted butter. Pour in the batter, and shake the pan a little so that the batter levels off. Reduce the heat to low, cover, and cook for 5 minutes. Carefully flip the omelet over to the other side, sneaking the remaining tablespoon of butter underneath. Cover again and cook for another 5 minutes.
4. Meanwhile, if you like, warm up a small frying pan over medium heat and then add the sliced ham to warm it. To serve, cut the puffy pancake into quarters, and serve with the ham.

TIPS > + +
Garnish not only makes a plate pretty, but it also can cover a multitude of sins. If your omelet comes out of the pan in less than perfect condition, just cover the broken area with a twisted orange slice or a tiny bunch of grapes.

"Cooking together brings families together."

EGG-STUFFED BREAD DINNER

Hard-boiled eggs are good for more than breakfast or making egg salad. In this recipe, they provide the protein for an easy and attractive meal. The eggs can be made ahead of time, which makes this a really fast last-minute meal. We like to add peas for color, but you could dice any leftover colorful vegetable in their place. You can also replace half the eggs with ¾ cup of diced cooked ham.

You can use the bread you remove from the inside of the loaf to make croutons or bread crumbs at another time, or for poultry stuffing. Put it in a plastic bag, squeeze out the excess air, and freeze the bread for later use.

4 ¢
SERVINGS

6   tablespoons butter
¼   cup all-purpose flour
2½ cups milk
½   pound button mushrooms, sliced
½   cup frozen peas, thawed
1   teaspoon salt
⅛   teaspoon freshly ground black pepper
6   hard-boiled large eggs, peeled and sliced ½ inch thick
1   large round loaf French or Italian bread, unsliced
2   or 3 strips pimiento, diced, for garnish (optional)

1. In a medium pot over low heat, melt the butter. Transfer 2 tablespoons to a cup and set aside. Add the flour to the remaining butter in the pot and stir over medium-low heat until blended. Gradually add the milk, stir until it begins to thicken, and let simmer until the flour loses its raw taste, about 3 minutes.

2. Add the mushrooms, peas, salt, and pepper to the pot and simmer until the mushrooms are cooked, about 3 minutes. Add the sliced eggs and simmer until heated through.

3. Meanwhile, slice the top off the round loaf, about an inch down from the top; save the slice for the "lid." Scoop out the bread inside, leaving a 1-inch-thick layer all around the "bowl." Brush the insides of the loaf with the reserved 2 tablespoons melted butter. Fill the loaf with the warm egg-vegetable mixture, and pour the sauce over it. Garnish with the pimiento, if desired, and replace the top to serve.

4. Serve by scooping out the contents of the bread "bowl" onto plates, and then let people break off pieces of the bread.

PIZZA FRITTATA

A frittata is just an omelet that's baked in the oven, so it doesn't need to be folded. Once you get the hang of making frittatas, feel free to experiment with any ingredients you'd use for regular omelets. This version looks like pizza, which is great for persuading kids who think they don't like eggs to give it a try! If you're serving adults, you can substitute dill for the parsley. Serve this with a simple salad or some green veggies.

4 SERVINGS ¢

3   tablespoons olive oil
½   cup thinly sliced onion
8   large eggs
¼   cup freshly grated
      Parmesan cheese
1   small clove garlic, chopped
1   tablespoon chopped fresh
      parsley
1   teaspoon salt
¼   teaspoon freshly ground
      black pepper
1   tomato, thinly sliced
2   ounces thinly sliced
      pepperoni

1. Preheat the oven to 350°F.
2. Heat the oil in a 10-inch ovenproof skillet over medium heat. Add the onion and cook, stirring, until tender and golden, about 5 minutes.
3. Meanwhile, in a large bowl, beat the eggs with 2 tablespoons water. Add the cheese, garlic, parsley, salt, and pepper and beat until well blended. Pour into the skillet with the cooked onion and reduce the heat to low.
4. Cook the eggs, lifting the edges and tilting the pan so that the excess liquid on top can cook, until they set, about 2 minutes. When the egg mixture is no longer runny but still looks wet, turn off the heat and decorate the top with the sliced tomato and pepperoni. Transfer the skillet to the oven and bake for 8 minutes, or until the top of the eggs is set.
5. To serve, loosen the edges of the frittata with a spatula and slide out onto a large plate. Cut into wedges to serve.

> With some imagination you can rustle up a last-minute meal anytime there are eggs around.

BRUNCH-FOR-DINNER CASSEROLE

Make this in the morning to be ready for dinner, or at night to serve for brunch the next day. It needs to be assembled and then refrigerated for about 8 hours. Then all you need to do is bake it. It looks beautiful and there's only one dish to clean. I like to serve this with some fresh fruit on the side—a bunch of grapes, sliced mango or papaya, or cinnamon apples.

4-6 ¢ SERVINGS

1½ teaspoons butter
6 slices white or whole wheat bread, cubed
8 ounces cheddar cheese
¾ pound bulk sausage, sausage patties, or bacon, cooked, drained, and crumbled
6 large eggs
2 cups milk
¾ teaspoon dry mustard
1 cup thinly sliced button mushrooms

1. Lightly grease a 2-quart casserole dish. Spread the bread cubes evenly over the bottom. Coarsely grate the cheese over the bread cubes. Sprinkle the crumbled meat over the cheese.

2. In a medium-size bowl, beat together the eggs, milk, and mustard. Pour over the contents of the casserole. Cover and refrigerate for at least 8 hours or overnight.

3. Preheat the oven to 325°F.

4. Sprinkle the mushrooms evenly across the top of the casserole. Bake for 1 hour and 15 minutes, or until puffy and golden brown on top. Remove from the oven and let rest for about 10 minutes. Scoop to serve.

TARTIFLETTE POTATO QUICHE

A *tartiflette* is a French country dish that's similar to a quiche. While it can't be called low-fat, considering the bacon, butter, cheese, and cream, it uses potatoes for the crust rather than pastry (and the pastry is the highest-fat and most caloric part of any pie). Feel free to experiment with other flavors; for example, use ham instead of bacon, or make a vegetarian version by adding sautéed spinach. Serve it with a simple mixed green salad.

 $

4 SERVINGS

2   pounds all-purpose potatoes, peeled
1   tablespoon butter
2   medium onions, finely chopped
½   pound bacon, diced
⅛   teaspoon salt
    Freshly ground black pepper
12 ounces Gruyère or Jarlsberg cheese, coarsely grated (about 3 cups)
1   cup heavy cream

1. Preheat the oven to 350°F.
2. Add the potatoes to a large pot with enough water to cover. Bring to a boil and simmer for 5 to 8 minutes, depending on their size; the potatoes should be cooked through, but not mushy. Drain, let cool, and thinly slice.
3. Melt the butter in a skillet over medium heat. Add the onions and bacon and cook, stirring, until the bacon is well cooked. Drain off the fat and set aside.
4. Lightly coat the inside of an 8-inch quiche dish, pie plate, or tart pan with nonstick cooking spray.

Using half the potatoes, arrange them in overlapping slices to cover the bottom and sides of the dish. Sprinkle with the salt and several healthy grindings of pepper.
5. Spread the bacon-onion mixture over the potatoes, then sprinkle with half the cheese. Cover with another overlapping layer of the remaining potatoes and pour the cream evenly over the top. Sprinkle with the remaining cheese. Bake for about 30 minutes, or until the top is a golden-brown firm crust.
6. Cut as you would a pie and serve in slices.

SUPER DUPER SCRAMBLER

This is one of the easiest meals you can make. Just go through your refrigerator and see what frozen or already cooked veggies you've got. Then add some leftover meat or lunch meat and/or some cheese, and you're ready. Be creative. I give the basic recipe here, but you just want a total of 1 cup of diced stuff for every 4 eggs. Some of the combinations I've tried include leftover meatballs, chopped tomatoes, and peppers with oregano; salami, chicken, and broccoli with Parmesan cheese; and ham, pineapple, and spinach. If you're using frozen vegetables, cook them first; similarly, sauté onions or peppers first. Mushrooms and tomatoes can be added without prior cooking; and cheeses, if used, should be added about halfway through.

4 ¢
SERVINGS

2   teaspoons butter
2   tablespoons chopped onion
2   cups total diced, cooked
     meat and/or vegetables
¼   teaspoon dried herbs
     or spices, as seems
     appropriate
8   large eggs beaten with 2
     teaspoons water
     Salt and freshly ground
     black pepper
4   to 8 slices bread, toasted

1. Melt the butter in a large frying pan (or, if you like softer scrambled eggs, in the top of a double boiler over boiling water) over medium heat. Add the onion and cook, stirring, until it is soft and golden, about 2 minutes. Add any ingredients that need cooking (raw peppers, for example) and cook briefly, stirring. Add the rest of the meat and/or vegetables and cook, stirring, until heated through.

2. Mix the herbs or spices of your choosing into the beaten eggs. Pour the eggs over the ingredients in the pan and cook, stirring, until set and scrambled. Season to taste with salt and pepper. Serve over toast.

SCRUMPTIOUS

SALADS

"There are no rules when it comes to making a salad."

There are many ways of creating a good salad, and I truly feel the best way is to add your own personal taste to it. There are no rules when it comes to making a salad.

Only you know the perfect combination of ingredients that make a salad so "mmm-mmm good" to you.

My son is a big salad lover. He will eat almost a whole serving bowl of salad in one sitting—and I'm not talking about a single-serving bowl either! He likes his salad with plenty of lettuce and cucumber. Our favorite dressing is very simple—a splash of lemon juice, a small packet of herbal dressing mix, some chopped cilantro, a pinch of salt and pepper, and a dash of olive oil.

I'm also a big believer in using local produce. Whenever possible, use vegetables straight from the garden rather than store-bought. If you don't have a garden, go to your nearest produce market or roadside stand and buy fresh. There is no comparison between fresh garden tomatoes and those that have traveled a long distance (and have probably been either bred for dura-bility rather than flavor or treated to look red when they're not even ripe). Using local vegetables in season is also an environmentally friendly thing to do, as it cuts down on the trucking needed to stock our stores with seasonal fruits and veggies all year 'round.

Salads are so healthy—except when they're not. Too many people really think of salad only as a vehicle for some yummy salad dressing. Did you know that eating a good salad with a fattening dressing can be just as bad, calorie-wise and fat-wise, as eating a fast-food burger? Many people eat salads when dieting only to discover they don't lose the weight they thought they would because they pile on the high-fat Caesar or blue cheese dressing.

All sorts of great flavored vinegars are available these days, and they're perfect for making healthy vinaigrettes. Try whisking together some balsamic vinegar or rasp-berry vinegar with a little olive oil, which is good for you in moderation. A French trick is to whip in a little dry mustard, which helps bind it together and makes it seem thicker. And by all means, whisk in some fresh herbs, too.

For a little crunch, toss a handful of nuts or seeds over your salad; both are good sources of protein and nutrients. Try to avoid croutons or taco strips, which are usually fried. A little grated cheese is tasty too, but can add a lot of fat, so use it in moderation.

Salads, of course, don't have to be green. You'll find all sorts of healthy main-course salads in this chapter with interesting ingredients such as chicken, pasta, chickpeas, and more. Get inspired! And remember that you can turn any of these recipes into a side salad by making half as much and going a little heavier on the greens.

TIPS > + +
Whenever possible, use vegetables straight from the garden rather than store-bought. If you don't have a garden, go to your nearest produce market or roadside stand and buy fresh.

MANDARIN CHICKEN AND WALNUT SALAD

This salad is sophisticated enough to satisfy adults, but its sweetness and crunch give it kid appeal, too.

4 **¢**
SERVINGS

6 to 8 cups mixed greens
   (or two 10.5-ounce
   packages)
1½ cups mandarin orange
   segments, drained
½ red onion, thinly sliced
½ pound grilled or broiled
   chicken, thinly sliced (or
   2 cups cubed)
½ cup olive oil
3 tablespoons balsamic
   vinegar
½ teaspoon salt
¼ teaspoon freshly ground
   black pepper
½ cup chopped walnuts

1. In a large bowl, toss together the greens, oranges, and onion.
2. Put the chicken on a plate and microwave until heated through, about 1 minute on high. Add to the salad.

3. In a separate bowl, whisk together the oil, vinegar, salt, and pepper. Pour over the salad and toss well. Sprinkle with the walnuts and serve immediately.

PARADISE PAPAYA-CHICKEN SALAD

Papaya is a great digestive aid, plus I love the flavor. Papaya and mango both make any meal feel tropical, and they can also substitute for each other if one isn't to your liking. If you can't find reasonably priced tropical fruit in your market, or you haven't acquired the taste, you can substitute cantaloupe or honeydew melon for the papaya and ripe peaches for the mango.

4 SERVINGS ¢

¼   **cup canola oil**
1   **teaspoon grated fresh ginger**
2   **teaspoons minced garlic**
2   **boneless, skinless chicken breast halves (10 to 12 ounces total)**
¼   **cup orange juice**
¼   **cup white wine vinegar**
2   **tablespoons olive oil**
6   **to 8 cups mixed salad greens (or two 10.5-ounce packages)**
1   **papaya, peeled and diced**
1   **mango, sliced into wedges**
1   **red bell pepper, seeded and sliced**

1. Heat the canola oil in a large skillet over medium heat. Add the ginger and 1 teaspoon of the garlic and cook, stirring, just until the garlic is golden, about 1 minute. Add the chicken and cook until it is white inside, 5 to 7 minutes. Remove from the heat.

2. In a medium-size mixing bowl or a container with a tight-fitting lid, combine the orange juice, vinegar, olive oil, and the remaining 1 teaspoon garlic. Mix or shake until well blended.

3. Arrange the salad greens on a large serving platter. Distribute the papaya, mango, and bell pepper evenly over the top. Top with the warm chicken and drizzle with the dressing.

 +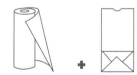

TIPS > Don't store fresh greens in the plastic bag they come in. Moisture will condense and cause them to rot. Remove greens from their bag and wrap in a paper towel or linen dishtowel, then put the wrapped greens in a paper bag (unless you have a special "salad keeper"). Only wash greens you are about to use, because you don't want to put them into the fridge wet. Store mushrooms this way, too.

MEDITERRANEAN CHICKPEA-PASTA SALAD

Chewy pasta shapes such as spiral rotini are great for pasta salads because their nooks and crannies really hold on to the dressing. Chickpeas, also known as garbanzo beans, are a significant source of protein in this meatless main-course salad.

4 SERVINGS ¢

6   ounces rotini pasta
3   tablespoons olive oil
2   tablespoons red or white wine vinegar
1   tablespoon chopped fresh oregano (or 1 teaspoon dried)
⅛   teaspoon salt
    Freshly ground black pepper
1   pound tomatoes, seeded and diced
1   15-ounce can chickpeas
1   2.5-ounce can sliced black olives, drained (optional)
1   large cucumber, seeded and chopped
3   scallions or chives, thinly sliced (discard darkest green parts)
6   to 8 cups mixed salad greens (or two 10.5-ounce packages)
4   ounces crumbled feta cheese

1. Cook the pasta according to the package directions. Drain and rinse under cold running water to stop further cooking. Set aside.

2. In a small bowl, mix together the oil, vinegar, oregano, salt, and a few grinds of pepper. In another bowl, toss together the tomatoes, chickpeas, the olives, if desired, the cucumber, and the scallions.

3. Arrange the salad greens in a large shallow bowl or on a serving platter and top with the cooked pasta. Layer the tomato-chickpea mixture on top of the pasta, then pour the dressing evenly over the top. Garnish with the crumbled feta.

TANGY BOSTON CLEMENTINE SALAD

Oh, my darling, Clementine—you may have a pretty name, but you can be replaced. Clementines are the smallest, sweetest variety of mandarin oranges, so if they're not available, you can easily use mandarins or tangerines in this recipe.

This also calls for Boston lettuce, which is a butterhead lettuce; you can use any lettuce from the soft-leafed butterhead family, including Buttercrunch and Bibb (and of course you won't be breaking any culinary laws if you use any other kind of lettuce or greens you prefer). We also like to use cremini (baby portobello) mushrooms in this salad, but feel free to use any other kind of mushroom that's handy or inexpensive, or whose flavor you prefer.

1   **pound Boston lettuce, leaves torn into bite-size pieces**
1   **cup shredded red cabbage**
2   **clementine oranges, peeled, pitted, and segmented**
1   **cup sliced cremini mushrooms, sliced**
1   **yellow bell pepper, seeded and diced**
1   **tablespoon plus 1 teaspoon olive oil**
2   **tablespoons balsamic vinegar**
1   **tablespoon Dijon mustard**
1   **teaspoon minced garlic**
¼   **cup sunflower seeds**

1. In a large bowl, combine the lettuce, cabbage, orange segments, mushrooms, and bell pepper. Toss well and arrange on individual serving plates.

2. In a small mixing bowl or a container with a tight-fitting lid, combine the oil, vinegar, mustard, and garlic. Mix or shake well to blend, then drizzle over each salad. Garnish with the sunflower seeds.

SPINACH-PINEAPPLE CHICKEN SALAD

This tasty salad can be made with leftover chicken or turkey, or with cooked shrimp, or even well-drained canned tuna. The pineapple can be fresh, or from any kind of canned pineapple—rings, cubes, or tidbits, well drained. And don't risk your knuckles by shredding the carrots on a grater; once you've peeled the carrots, just keep using the vegetable peeler to turn them into shreds. I don't bother to peel the cucumber, because it's sliced so thin, but if you don't like cucumber rind, feel free to peel it before slicing.

4 ¢
SERVINGS

5 cups fresh spinach leaves
2 large carrots, peeled and shredded
1 medium cucumber, thinly sliced
1 cup diced pineapple (if canned, drain first)
1 cup olive oil
⅓ cup red wine vinegar
2 teaspoons dried basil
1 teaspoon dried oregano
1 teaspoon salt
½ teaspoon freshly ground black pepper
2 cups diced cooked chicken

1. In a large bowl, toss together the spinach, carrots, cucumber, and pineapple.

2. In another bowl, whisk together the oil, vinegar, basil, oregano, salt, and pepper. Gently toss the dressing into the salad until the greens are well coated. Add the chicken, toss again, and serve immediately.

TURKEY, CRANBERRY, AND PISTACHIO SALAD

Turkey and cranberries—the all-American combination, given extra crunch by pears, celery, and nuts. Dried cranberries have concentrated sweetness; if they seem too dry, you can plump them up by soaking them in a little lukewarm water for a few minutes. We chose pistachio nuts for their unique flavor and greenish color, but you could just as easily substitute cashews or walnuts.

4 SERVINGS ¢

2   cups diced cooked turkey breast
1   pear, cored and diced
1   stalk celery, diced
½   cup dried cranberries
4   teaspoons coarsely chopped pistachio nuts
    Salt and freshly ground black pepper
12 large lettuce leaves
6   ounces fat-free plain or vanilla yogurt
1   tablespoon lime juice
1   teaspoon finely chopped fresh basil (or ½ teaspoon dried)
1   teaspoon finely chopped fresh parsley

1. In a medium-size bowl, combine the turkey, pear, celery, cranberries, and pistachios. Season with salt and pepper to taste.

2. Tear up the lettuce leaves into large pieces and put on individual serving plates. Put the turkey mixture on top of the lettuce.

3. In a small mixing bowl, combine the yogurt, lime juice, basil, and parsley, blending well. Drizzle the salads with the dressing and serve immediately.

E-Z SESAME-GINGER CHICKEN SALAD

My guest Esther Zaccone (E-Z, get it?) loves playing with ingredients to create fresh combinations; here she turns the ingredients one might expect to find in a stir-fry into a spicy salad. This can be topped with chow mein noodles for crunch, but Esther admits that she prefers to use canned french-fried onion rings!

SERVINGS $

6 tablespoons olive oil

1 tablespoon plus 1 teaspoon sesame oil

2 boneless, skinless chicken breast halves, cubed (½ to ¾ pound total)

4 cloves garlic, chopped

4 scallions, chopped (all but the darkest green parts)

1 tablespoon slivered almonds

2 tablespoons soy sauce

5 tablespoons ginger-teriyaki sauce

3 to 4 cups salad greens

1 plum tomato, diced

1 carrot, peeled and sliced

1 small bell pepper (any color), seeded and chopped

3 tablespoons balsamic vinegar

1 teaspoon light brown sugar
Salt and freshly ground black pepper

½ cup chow mein noodles (optional)

1. Heat 2 tablespoons of the olive oil with 1 tablespoon of the sesame oil in a wok or large skillet over medium-high heat. When the oil pops when a drop of water touches it, add the chicken, 1½ teaspoons of the garlic, half the scallions, and the almonds and cook, stirring, until the chicken is browned, 3 to 5 minutes. Add the soy sauce and 3 tablespoons of the ginger-teriyaki sauce to the wok and cook, stirring, to marry the flavors, 1 to 2 minutes more. Remove from the heat.

2. In a salad bowl, combine the greens, tomato, carrot, bell pepper, and the rest of the scallions. Arrange the hot chicken mixture on top of the salad, including the pan drippings.

3. In a mixing bowl or a container with a tight-fitting lid, combine the remaining 4 tablespoons olive oil, the vinegar, the remaining garlic, the remaining 2 tablespoons ginger-teriyaki sauce, the remaining 1 teaspoon sesame oil, and the brown sugar. Stir or shake well and adjust the seasoning with salt and pepper to taste.

4. Drizzle the dressing over the chicken salad and top with chow mein noodles, if desired. Serve immediately.

KEY LIME SCALLOP AND COUSCOUS SALAD

Delicious, different, and easy: Once you prepare the ingredients for this salad, putting it together is a snap. Prepare it well ahead of time at your convenience; you can chill it for as long as overnight. For a variation, substitute cooked peeled shrimp for the scallops.

4 $ SERVINGS

1 cup white wine
¾ pound bay scallops
1⅓ cups couscous
1½ pounds tomatoes, seeded and diced
1 cup diced cucumber
2 tablespoons diced red onion
1 tablespoon chopped fresh mint leaves
  Juice of 2 key limes
1 tablespoon olive oil
2 cups dark leafy greens

1. In a medium-size saucepan, combine the wine with 1 cup water and bring to a low boil. Add the scallops and cook until no longer translucent, about 1 minute. Drain and set aside to cool. Prepare the couscous according to the package directions.

2. In a large bowl, combine the scallops, cooked couscous, tomatoes, cucumber, onion, and mint. Add the lime juice and oil and mix well. Refrigerate for at least 2 hours.

3. Divide the greens among four plates. Top with equal portions of the couscous-scallop mixture and serve.

 + +

TIPS >
An easy and tasty way to quickly cook scallops or shrimp for use in salads is to poach them in a mixture of 1 cup of white wine and 1 cup of water.

CCG (CHICKEN, CASHEWS, AND GRAPES) SALAD

This delicious salad combines the flavor of moist poached chicken, cashews, and grapes in a light but filling meal. I like it with a fruity, low-fat raspberry vinaigrette, but any light dressing of your choice, such as honey and poppy seed, could work, too. Red grapes look prettier, I think, but any grapes are fine for flavor.

SERVINGS

4 **boneless, skinless chicken breast halves**
1 **cup white wine and/or chicken broth**
8 **cups mixed salad greens**
¾ **cup low-fat raspberry vinaigrette**
2 **cups seedless grapes**
½ **cup roasted cashews**

1. In a deep frying pan or large pot, cover the chicken breasts with the white wine plus enough water to cover thoroughly. Cover, with the lid slightly ajar, and simmer until the chicken is no longer pink inside, about 10 minutes. Drain the chicken, cool, and cut into 1-inch cubes.

2. Toss the salad greens with the vinaigrette. Add the chicken, grapes, and cashews and toss lightly.

HOT SMOKED TURKEY-GOUDA SALAD

This can of course be made with chicken, too. We like the smoky flavor that using smoked cheese adds, but you can use unsmoked cheese instead. Another option would be to use plain cheese and smoked turkey. You can also combine the ingredients without cooking them and serve this cold.

SERVINGS

1½ **cups cubed cooked turkey**
2 **stalks celery, thinly sliced (about ¾ cup)**
1 **small onion, diced**
⅔ **cup (6 ounces) low-fat mayonnaise or salad dressing such as Miracle Whip**
2 **teaspoons lemon juice**
¼ **teaspoon salt**
2 **tablespoons pine nuts or sliced almonds (optional)**
½ **cup cubed smoked Gouda cheese (about 6 ounces)**
1 **cup croutons or cubed toasted bread**
Lettuce or mixed salad greens for serving

1. In a large metal bowl or the top of a double-boiler, combine the turkey, celery, onion, mayonnaise, lemon juice, and salt. Add the nuts, if desired, for crunch. Place the bowl over a pot of water over low heat and heat the turkey mixture until it begins to bubble, or is heated through and well blended.

2. Remove from the heat and immediately stir in the cheese. Stir in the croutons. Serve warm over the lettuce.

VERSATILE
and
VEGETARIAN

"It's always good to have some
vegetarian dishes in your repertoire."

Vegetarian (no-meat) meals are a staple of the everyday diet in many countries from India to Africa, as well as in many others where people eat meat only rarely. While

vegetarian meals tend to be quite healthy and nutritious, don't make the mistake of automatically considering them an all-you-can-eat buffet; cheese and nuts are often used to provide the protein, and both are high in fat.

A lot of kids go through a vegetarian phase, but often that just means they won't eat meat; they might even accept fish. Some vegetarians (vegans) are stricter and won't eat anything that breathes or that comes from animals that breathe. That rules out seafood, dairy products, and eggs. Ovo-lacto vegetarians will eat eggs and milk products, including cheese.

It's always good to have some vegetarian dishes in your repertoire. That way, you won't panic when your teenagers announce they've become vegetarians or

when a vegetarian guest comes for dinner. It's easy enough to add some meat or cheese to most vegetarian recipes, if you need to cater to a mixed crowd, or to use a main course for one person as a side dish for the rest. And there's the added advantage that since protein sources are generally the most expensive element of a meal, downplaying them can really help slash your food budget.

Becoming a vegetarian is something I sometimes aspire to; it seems so healthy and natural. I enjoy fish and chicken and a good steak too much, but I also love many vegetarian meals: Indian dishes with the spices and curries that make them so delicious, flavorful, and colorful; stir-fries that seem so crisp and fresh; Italian dishes so good that "where's the meat?"

never crosses your mind; plus all the tasty dishes developed in the Caribbean, Latin America, and the Middle East in times of meat scarcity that have since become part of their culinary traditions.

For those considering becoming vegetarians—or who are parents of one—do your research into the pros and cons of such a diet. Study the nutritional values of the foods and find the combinations that work for you. Make sure to always eat healthfully, with enough sources of iron and protein and without an overabundance of calories from fat (those nuts can really add up fast). Any drastic change in eating habits can also affect health, so it's always wise to speak with a doctor, pediatrician, dietitian, or nutritionist if you decide to "go vegan."

FALAFEL PITAS WITH HUMMUS

Sometimes called "Middle Eastern meatballs," falafel is one of those great vegetarian dishes that has easy appeal for meat-eaters. It is usually deep-fried; using canola oil means that it will have minimal saturated fat, but if you are really watching all kinds of fat, there is an oven-baked variation.

Hummus is available already prepared in most stores, but it's a lot less expensive to make it yourself in quantity (you have to buy the tahini paste to make even a little hummus, so you might as well use it and make a lot). Once it's made, hummus can be refrigerated for up to three days or frozen for up to a month. You may find you need to stir in a drop or two more of olive oil when you defrost it.

4 SERVINGS $

1 **16-ounce bag dried chickpeas** (aka garbanzo beans)
1 **medium onion, chopped**
3 **tablespoons chopped fresh parsley**
3 **cloves garlic, chopped**
1 **teaspoon ground coriander**
1 **teaspoon ground cumin**
  Salt and freshly ground black pepper
½ **teaspoon baking powder**
  Canola oil for frying

For Hummus:
1 **14.5-ounce can chickpeas, drained**
⅓ **cup lemon juice (or juice of 2 medium lemons)**
3 **tablespoons tahini (sesame seed paste, sold in the international section of most markets)**
1 **clove garlic, halved**
½ **teaspoon salt**
¼ **teaspoon ground cumin**
  Olive oil
1 **tablespoon chopped fresh parsley (optional)**
2 **large tomatoes, thinly sliced**
4 **pita pockets (preferably whole wheat)**

1. Rinse the dried chickpeas and soak them in enough water to cover overnight, until softened. Drain and add to a saucepan with 2 cups fresh water. Bring to a boil, then simmer for 15 minutes. Drain and let cool.
2. In a blender or food processor, combine the cooked chickpeas, onion, parsley, garlic, coriander, and cumin. Add salt and pepper to taste, then add the baking powder. Blend into a smooth, thick paste. Form the mixture into small golf ball–size balls, flattening them slightly so they don't roll.
3. Add enough canola oil to a large skillet to fry the falafel (about 2 inches should do) and set over medium-high heat. When the oil is hot, carefully add the falafel balls and fry until crisp and deep golden brown, about 2 minutes per side. Drain on paper towels to absorb the excess oil. Alternatively, to bake in the oven: Preheat the oven to 475°F.

Spray a baking sheet with nonstick cooking spray. Place the falafel on the tray and bake for 10 minutes.
4. Prepare the hummus: Add the chickpeas, lemon juice, tahini, garlic, salt, and cumin to a blender. Process until the mixture is smooth, adding a little water if the hummus is too thick. Transfer to a small serving dish and drizzle a little olive oil on top. Garnish with the chopped parsley, if desired. This makes 2 cups of hummus.
5. Add 2 tablespoonfuls of the hummus and some sliced tomatoes to each pita pocket. Add the hot falafel balls and serve with additional hummus on the side. (If using the oven-baked version, chop the tomatoes instead of slicing them and retain their juices. After you've put the falafel into the pitas, cover them with the juicy chopped tomatoes to counter any dryness the oven-baked version can have.)

FIESTA CORNBREAD PIE

This is a quick dish to prepare, but allow an hour before you're going to eat since it needs time in the oven. You can substitute canned corn kernels for the fresh or frozen corn; drain them well and add them only after the other ingredients are cooked. If you buy dried kidney beans to use instead of the canned beans called for in the recipe, soak and precook them according to the package directions before using.

SERVINGS 4 $

1 onion, diced
2 cups fresh or frozen corn kernels
1 red bell pepper, seeded and chopped
1 cup tomato sauce
1 small can green chiles, chopped
2 tablespoons chili powder
4 cups canned kidney beans, rinsed, drained, and mashed
1 6.5-ounce package cornbread mix

1. Preheat the oven to 350°F.
2. Add the onion and 2 tablespoons water to a large skillet over medium heat and cook, stirring occasionally, until the onion is softened, 4 to 6 minutes. Add the corn, bell pepper, tomato sauce, green chiles, and chili powder and cook, stirring occasionally, for 5 minutes. Reduce the heat to low, stir in the mashed beans, and cook for 10 minutes more.
3. Pour the bean mixture into a lightly greased 9 x 13-inch baking dish. Prepare the cornbread mix batter according to the package directions and spread it over the beans. Bake for about 45 minutes, or until the cornbread is golden. Cut into squares to serve.

TIPS >
Use fresh corn when it's in season (and thus least expensive). Three ears of corn will yield about 1½ cups of corn kernels. Boil or steam the corn on the cob, and then remove the kernels to use in recipes or as a side dish.

RATATOUILLE WITH COUSCOUS

We tend to think of ratatouille as French or Italian and couscous as Middle Eastern, but they are both Mediterranean dishes and they go well together. Packaged couscous comes in several varieties, usually all the same price as plain; the plain, garlic, or pine nut varieties would go best with this dish.

4 SERVINGS ¢

1   **10-ounce box couscous**
2   **tablespoons olive oil**
1   **green bell pepper, chopped**
1   **medium onion, chopped**
1   **clove garlic, crushed**
6   **large tomatoes, seeded and diced**
1   **medium eggplant, peeled and cubed**
2   **small green zucchini, sliced**
1   **teaspoon salt (optional)**
¼   **teaspoon freshly ground black pepper**

1. Cook the couscous according to the package directions.

2. While the couscous is cooking, heat the oil in a large pot over medium-high heat. Add the bell pepper, onion, and garlic and cook, stirring, until softened, about 5 minutes. Add the tomatoes, eggplant, zucchini, salt if desired, and black pepper. Cook, stirring occasionally, until the vegetables are tender, about 10 minutes.

3. Serve the ratatouille over the couscous.

BARLEY AND APPLE PILAF

This is a great variation on the typical rice pilaf, and the fruit helps to make it a main course kids will enjoy. For protein, you can add some pine nuts or peanuts, or for meat-eaters, add some diced cooked chicken.

Cilantro is the name more commonly used in the United States and Mexico for fresh coriander, as it's known in other parts of the world. In America, we tend to refer to the fresh leaves as cilantro and the dried seeds (sold whole and ground) as coriander, but they're all from the same plant.

4 ¢
SERVINGS

2   tablespoons butter
½   cup barley
¼   cup finely chopped onion
1   10-ounce can chicken broth
⅓   cup raisins
¼   teaspoon dried oregano
2   large cooking apples
        (Granny Smith or similar),
        cored and finely chopped
1   stalk celery, chopped
2   tablespoons chopped fresh
        cilantro (or, if you must,
        2 teaspoons ground
        coriander)

1. Melt the butter over medium heat in a large skillet. Add the barley and onion and cook, stirring, until the onion is golden, 3 to 5 minutes. Add the broth, raisins, and oregano; bring to a boil, then reduce the heat to a simmer. Cover and cook until the barley is tender and the liquid is absorbed, about 45 minutes. **2.** Add the apples, celery, and cilantro and cook for 5 minutes more. (If using ground coriander, hold off adding until the last 2 minutes of cooking.) Ladle into bowls to serve.

TIPS >
Don't forget to check the lowest grocery-store shelves; that's where you'll often find the best values.

MEXICAN BLACK BEANS AND RICE

Beans and rice is a staple in many cultures—and it's so good for you. Lots of protein, lots of fiber, and lots of good taste! For a non-vegetarian variation, instead of the green pepper you can cook an Italian sausage link in a little olive oil for about 5 minutes, slice it, and stir it into the cooked beans and rice.

4 SERVINGS ¢

¼ cup olive oil
1½ teaspoons minced garlic
1 small onion, chopped
1 green bell pepper, seeded and diced
1 13-ounce can black beans, rinsed and drained
1 teaspoon dried oregano
1 package Sazón seasoning, any variety (optional; see Note)
  Salt and freshly ground black pepper
2 cups hot cooked white rice

1. Heat the oil in a large skillet over medium heat. Add the garlic and cook, stirring, until it's fragrant, 1 to 2 minutes. Add the onion and bell pepper and cook, stirring, until the pepper pieces are tender, about 3 minutes longer. Add the black beans, oregano, and Sazón seasoning. Add salt and black pepper to taste. Simmer, covered, for about 30 minutes.
2. Serve the bean mixture over the hot rice.

Note: Sazón is a Latino-style seasoned salt made by Goya. You can approximate it by combining a teaspoon of salt with a pinch of ground coriander.

"JA MON" JAMAICAN RICE AND PEAS

Pigeon peas are a roundish bean commonly used in the food of many cultures. Called *toor*, they can be the main ingredient in the Indian food *dal*; in East Africa, pigeon peas are called *gunga* peas. You can often find canned pigeon peas in the international section of the supermarket, or you can substitute kidney beans or black-eyed peas.

4 ¢
SERVINGS

1   **16-ounce can pigeon peas, drained and liquid reserved**
1   **habanero chile, chopped, or**
3   **jalapeño chiles, seeded and chopped**
1   **teaspoon minced garlic**
1½ **cups unsweetened coconut milk**
1   **cup white rice**
½   **medium onion (preferably Vidalia), chopped**
1   **teaspoon dried thyme**
    Salt and freshly ground black pepper

1. Add the pigeon peas, chiles, and garlic to a large skillet over medium heat. Measure the reserved bean liquid; add to the coconut milk along with enough water to make 2¼ cups of liquid in total. Add the liquid to the bean mixture and stir to combine.

2. Add the rice, onion, and thyme to the skillet and stir to combine; raise the heat and bring to a boil. Reduce the heat, cover, and simmer until all the liquid is absorbed, about 20 minutes. Season with salt and pepper to taste, and serve.

THAI YELLOW VEGETABLE CURRY

A key ingredient of Thai curry is curry paste (in this case, yellow curry paste), which can be found in some markets, Asian markets, or online. There is really no good substitute for it, so if you can't find it, file this recipe away until you can. You can make your own, but it's complicated and requires a lot of ingredients.

4 SERVINGS ¢

3 large potatoes, peeled and cubed

3 tablespoons yellow curry paste (see headnote)

1 tablespoon canola oil

1 22.5-ounce can coconut milk

1 head broccoli, chopped (tough stems saved for making slaw or discarded)

1 8-ounce bag frozen baby green peas

1 4-ounce can water chestnuts, drained

2 cups hot cooked white rice, preferably jasmine

1. Add the potatoes to a large pot and fill with water to cover. Bring to a boil and cook until tender, about 10 minutes. Drain off the water so that the potatoes do not continue cooking, but leave the potatoes in the pot.

2. Add the curry paste and oil to a large skillet over medium heat and cook, stirring constantly with a wire whisk, for about 1 minute. Stir in the coconut milk. Add the contents of the skillet to the drained potatoes.

3. Add the broccoli, peas, and water chestnuts to the pot. Cook over medium heat, covered, until the broccoli is tender, about 5 minutes.

4. Serve the curry over the rice.

BOK CHOY–SHIITAKE JAPANESE STIR-FRY

Since shiitake mushrooms are not always available fresh, this recipe uses the more commonly available dried version, which has the added advantage of providing more intense flavor.

SERVINGS

6 whole dried shiitake mushrooms
1 teaspoon minced garlic
1 teaspoon minced fresh ginger
2 cups chicken broth
1 cup canned sliced water chestnuts, drained
1 scallion, thinly sliced
1 tablespoon soy sauce
2 teaspoons cornstarch
1 large head bok choy
2 cups hot cooked white rice

1. Pour 1 cup boiling water over the shiitake mushrooms in a medium-size bowl and allow them to sit, covered, for 30 minutes to rehydrate. Trim off the mushroom stems, and reserve the soaking liquid.

2. Add the mushroom-soaking liquid to a large skillet. Add the garlic and ginger to the liquid in the skillet and simmer over medium heat for 2 minutes. Add the broth, water chestnuts, mushrooms, scallion, and soy sauce and simmer for 10 minutes.

3. Meanwhile, in a small bowl, stir the cornstarch together with 1/2 cup cold water; set aside.

4. Trim the bottom off the bok choy and discard; coarsely chop the rest. You should have about 4 cups of chopped bok choy. Place a steamer basket inside a pot, add water to the bottom of the pot, and bring to a boil. Add the bok choy to the steamer basket and steam, tossing occasionally, until barely tender, about 4 minutes. Add the steamed bok choy to the skillet and stir briefly. Stir in the cornstarch mixture and simmer until the liquid is thickened.

5. Serve over the rice.

PORTOBELLO
BURGERS

Have you ever noticed how portobello mushrooms look sort of like hamburger buns? Here's a vegetarian dish that not only replaces the meat, but the bun, too! Use medium-size instead of large mushrooms for a lunch version. And if you're serving kids, there's no law that says you can't replace the fresh mozzarella with American cheese. If you really get into the faux-burger routine, you can also cut up some parsnips or jícama into french-fry shapes and mix a little hot sauce into some strawberry jam for the "ketchup."

SERVINGS 4 $

6 **tablespoons olive oil**
  Juice of 2 medium lemons (or 6 tablespoons lemon juice)
2 **teaspoons minced garlic**
½ **teaspoon salt**
½ **teaspoon freshly ground black pepper**
8 **large portobello mushroom caps, stems removed**
1 **tablespoon finely chopped fresh oregano (or 1 teaspoon dried)**
6 **ounces Gruyère, Swiss, or Parmesan cheese, shredded or coarsely grated (about 1½ cups)**
2 **large tomatoes**
  Lettuce
8 **ounces fresh mozzarella cheese**

1. Preheat the broiler.

2. In a small bowl, whisk together 4 tablespoons of the oil with the lemon juice, garlic, salt, and pepper. Use a pastry brush (or a brand-new paintbrush, or a plastic bag with your hand inside) to coat both sides of the mushroom caps with the oil mixture; the caps will absorb it unevenly if you dip them into the bowl.

3. Place the caps, gill-side down, on a baking sheet or broiler tray at least 4 inches from the heating element and broil for 3 minutes. Remove the entire pan from the oven, leaving the broiler on. Flip over the mushroom caps and top each with an equal amount of the oregano and then of the shredded Gruyère. Return to the broiler and broil until the cheese melts, 2 to 3 minutes. While that's cooking, cut the tomatoes into thick (¼- to ½-inch) slices.

4. Place one of the mushroom caps on each of four plates. Top each with, in this order, some lettuce leaves, enough slices of tomato to cover the mushroom cap, and one-quarter of the mozzarella. Sprinkle with the remaining olive oil. Top each with the 4 remaining mushroom caps.

ALL-SEASON PUMPKIN STEW

Pumpkin is such a great vegetable that it's a shame most people only associate it with autumn. It's chock-full of vitamins, minerals, nutrients, and—as you might guess from the color—the antioxidant beta carotene. This overgrown member of the squash/gourd family is rich and meaty and makes such a good stew that you'll never be left wondering, "Where's the meat?" Our pumpkin stew is also quick and easy to make—any time of year. Try it with other winter squashes such as butternut or acorn, too. Serve with crusty bread.

SERVINGS 4 ¢

- 2 tablespoons olive oil
- 1 large Vidalia onion, chopped
- 1 tablespoon grated fresh ginger
- 2 teaspoons minced garlic
- 2 10.5-ounce cans vegetable broth
- 2 cups 1-inch cubes fresh pumpkin
- 3 medium yellow squash, sliced 1 inch thick
- 8 large carrots, sliced ½ inch thick
- 2 red bell peppers, seeded and sliced lengthwise
- 2 cups fresh green beans, ends trimmed and cut into 2-inch segments
- 1 bay leaf
  Salt and freshly ground black pepper

1. Heat the oil in a large heavy pot over medium heat. Add the onion, ginger, and garlic and cook, stirring, until the onion is tender, 5 to 7 minutes. Add the broth, pumpkin, squash, carrots, bell peppers, green beans, and bay leaf. Add salt and black pepper to taste and stir well. Bring to a rolling boil, reduce the heat to medium-low, cover, and cook, stirring occasionally to prevent sticking, until a chunky stew consistency is reached, about 45 minutes.

2. Remove the bay leaf and serve in bowls.

TOFU-PESTO PASTA

No vegetarian recipe collection would be complete without at least one tofu recipe. This highly nutritious vegetable-protein source, made from soybeans, has an unfair reputation for being bland—or rather, to be fair, it is bland, but because of that has a chameleon-like quality that lets it adapt to a variety of recipes in place of meat or cheese. Here, we've turned it into a healthy, low-fat, creamy sauce for pasta.

Because of the subtle flavor of this dish, we recommend avoiding strongly flavored mushrooms. Try button mushrooms or creminis (baby bellas). However, if someone you're feeding is really craving meat, you can chop up one or two large, meaty portobello mushroom caps.

8 ounces fusilli, gemelli, or penne pasta
¾ cup fresh basil
3 tablespoons olive oil
6 ounces soft tofu
¼ cup freshly grated Parmesan cheese
2 tablespoons lemon juice
1½ teaspoons minced garlic
¼ teaspoon salt
⅛ teaspoon freshly ground black pepper
½ pound button or cremini mushrooms, sliced
2 tablespoons minced onion
1 tomato, seeded and diced

1. Cook the pasta according to the package directions, drain, and transfer to a large serving bowl.

2. Meanwhile, in a blender or food processor, process the basil with 1 tablespoon of the oil until blended. Add 1 more tablespoon of the oil, the tofu, Parmesan, lemon juice, garlic, salt, and pepper, and blend until smooth. Pour into a large skillet and warm over low heat.

3. In a separate skillet over medium heat, add the remaining 1 tablespoon oil. Add the mushrooms and onion and cook, stirring, until they have yielded their liquid and the onion is softened, 5 to 7 minutes. Toss into the pasta.

4. Add the tofu-pesto mixture to the pasta and toss well. Garnish with the diced tomatoes. Serve immediately.

SAVORY SOUPS
and
SANDWICHES

"Broaden your horizons by combining a deluxe soup with a simple sandwich, or a simple broth with an interesting sandwich."

I love all kinds of soup. Some of my favorites are chicken soup, miso soup, and Thai soups with a bit of spice to add the kick. With a simple salad and a piece of bread,

soup can be filling and nutritious all at the same time.

My son loves chicken soup. I add a bit of curry spice and some hot pepper and rice and maybe some noodles, and he's a happy young man. I also find it helpful to keep soup on hand in the freezer for those times when you get home late from work. Just thaw it out, heat it up, and dinner is ready. One thing I also love about soup is adding veggies, be they carrots or peas or cabbage. If you don't overcook the vegetables, it's a great way to get more of the vitamins and minerals we need. You can also change up your favorite soups by adding some cream to them or by pureeing them.

Sandwiches also can be real meals, if you put some thought into them. A lot of salad ingredients make for good sandwiches, and vice versa. We've extended the concept of sandwiches to include other quick handheld food we think of as more appropriate for lunch than dinner, such as quesadillas and panini.

We're not suggesting that you pair up these soups with these sandwiches to make a complete meal, necessarily; but broaden your horizons by combining a deluxe soup with a simple sandwich, or a simple broth with an interesting sandwich, and you've got a viable dinner alternative.

WILD WEST CHILI SOUP

A cross between a soup and a stew, this doesn't need a sandwich to make a meal; just serve with a side salad or some crusty bread and you're done. Combining canned and fresh ingredients gives you a fast, easy, and hearty meal.

4 SERVINGS ¢

¾ **pound lean ground beef**
2 **medium onions, chopped**
1 **teaspoon minced garlic**
1 **tablespoon chili powder**
1 **10.5-ounce can beef broth**
1 **28-ounce can diced tomatoes, undrained**
2 **10.5-ounce cans kidney beans, undrained**
4 **ounces cooked elbow macaroni**

1. Add the beef to a large heavy pot over medium heat and cook, breaking it up with the edge of a spatula, until it turns brown. Add the onions, garlic, and chili powder and cook, stirring occasionally, until the beef is cooked through and the onions are tender, 5 to 8 minutes. Pour or siphon off any fat.

2. Add the broth, tomatoes in their juice, beans in their liquid, and 2 cups water to the pot. Raise the heat and bring to a boil. Reduce the heat and simmer, stirring occasionally, until the kidney beans are very tender, about 20 minutes. Toward the end of the cooking, stir in the macaroni and simmer until it is heated through.

3. Ladle into bowls to serve.

"WHAT A CROCK" FISH CHOWDER

Whenever I'm preparing fresh fish, I cut off the oddly shaped pieces that would cook faster than the rest, put them in plastic sandwich bags, and stick them in the freezer. When I've collected about a pound's worth of these fish "odds and ends," it's time to make chowder—and you don't even have to thaw the fish! Long, slow cooking adds richness to this fish-and-potato soup.

We like the flavor that a little bacon gives to potato soup, but if you're avoiding fat, salt, or meat, you can brown the onion in some olive oil cooking spray instead.

4 SERVINGS

4   slices bacon, diced
1   medium onion, chopped
3   to 4 scallions
2   large potatoes, peeled and diced
1   pound fresh or frozen boneless fish, cut into small pieces
2   teaspoons salt
1   teaspoon freshly ground black or white pepper
1   12-ounce can evaporated milk

1. Add the bacon and onion to a large skillet over medium heat and cook, stirring, until the bacon is cooked and the onion is tender, about 10 minutes. Use a slotted spoon to transfer the bacon and onion to the crock of a 2-quart or larger slow cooker; discard the fat.

2. Slice the scallions into ¼-inch-thick rounds, discarding the very greenest parts. Reserve 1 tablespoon of the medium-green slices for garnish and add the rest to the crock. Cover the bottom of the crock with the potatoes and layer the fish atop the potatoes. Add ½ cup water and sprinkle with the salt and pepper. Cover and cook on the low setting until the potatoes break easily, 6 to 9 hours. Add the evaporated milk during the last hour of cooking. Stir thoroughly and adjust the seasonings to taste.

3. Ladle into bowls to serve and garnish with the reserved green scallion slices.

POTATO SOUP FLORENTINE

Anything "Florentine" means there's spinach it in some-where—and often cheese, too. This rich potato soup meets both of those criteria. Just throw the ingredients into a slow cooker and let it work its magic.

4 SERVINGS ¢

- 4 **medium russet potatoes, peeled and diced**
- 1 **small onion, chopped**
- 1 **smoked ham hock**
- 4 **cups chicken broth**
- 1 **teaspoon dry mustard**
- 1 **teaspoon seasoned salt**
- ½ **teaspoon freshly ground black pepper**
- 1 **9-ounce box frozen chopped spinach, thawed**
- 4 **ounces shredded Swiss cheese (about 1 cup; optional)**

1. Add the potatoes, onion, and ham hock to the crock of a 2-quart or larger slow cooker. Stir in the chicken broth, mustard, salt, and pepper. Cover and cook on low until the potatoes are tender, 8 to 10 hours.

2. Remove the ham hock, reserving any meat; discard the bones. Return the meat to the pot along with the spinach. Cover and cook on high for an additional 15 to 20 minutes.

3. Ladle soup into bowls to serve. Sprinkle the Swiss cheese on top, if desired.

CREAM OF ZUCCHINI SOUP

This five-ingredient soup is so rich and easy that it's become a regular in my repertoire. It comes in especially handy if your garden yields a bumper crop of zucchini, or whenever those zucchini you didn't get around to cooking start to get a little soft. Summer squash can be substituted for some or all of the zucchini. And for a spicy change of pace, try adding a half a tablespoon of curry powder in the first step.

For vegetarians, you can substitute vegetable broth for the chicken broth, although the flavor will be a bit less rich, so you may want to experiment with some additional spices.

This recipe can be made through Step 2 and frozen; simply return the frozen part to a pot and pick up where you left off when you're ready for soup!

4 ¢ SERVINGS

1⅓ tablespoons butter
1   cup chopped onion
8   medium zucchini, peeled and sliced
4   cups chicken broth
     Seasoned salt and freshly ground black pepper
1   pint light cream or half-and-half

1. Melt the butter in a medium-size pot over medium heat. Add the onion and cook, stirring, until it becomes translucent, 3 to 5 minutes, being careful not to burn the butter. Add the zucchini and broth and bring to a boil. Reduce the heat, cover, and simmer until the zucchini is soft but not limp, 3 to 5 minutes.
2. Carefully pour the contents of the pot into a blender and puree until smooth.
3. Add seasoned salt and pepper to taste. Add the cream and blend on low speed until thoroughly blended. If the mixture has cooled, pour back into the pot to reheat; otherwise, pour directly into serving dishes.

"With a simple salad and a piece of bread soup, can be filling and nutritious all at the same time."

HEALTHY MUSHROOM-LEEK SOUP

This soup tastes rich and creamy but is actually low in fat. Make sure you use at least some dried mushrooms for deeper flavor. I like this soup thick and chunky, served with crusty bread, but you can also puree it after it's done to make a rich bisque.

SERVINGS

8   ounces dried shiitake mushrooms
1   cup chopped leeks (white parts only)
2   tablespoons all-purpose flour or cornstarch
⅛   teaspoon curry powder
2   cups skim milk
1   beef or vegetable bouillon cube
½   pound portobello or cremini mushrooms
    Salt and freshly ground black pepper

1. Add the dried mushrooms to a bowl with 1 cup hot water and let sit to rehydrate for at least 30 minutes. Trim off and discard the stems, and reserve the soaking liquid.

2. Coat the inside of a medium-size heavy pot with nonstick cooking spray and set over medium heat. Add the leeks to the pot and cook, stirring frequently, until they go limp, about 3 minutes. Sprinkle the leeks with the flour and the curry powder and stir. Gradually add the milk, stirring constantly. Add the bouillon cube.

3. Trim off and discard the woody parts of the fresh mushroom stems and coarsely chop the fresh mushrooms into chunks. Add to the pot, raise the heat to medium-high, and bring to a boil. Add the rehydrated mushrooms, including the soaking liquid, and return to a boil. Add salt and pepper to taste. Reduce the heat and simmer until the soup has thickened to a just-pourable consistency, 10 to 12 minutes; adjust seasoning as needed.

4. Ladle into soup bowls to serve.

CHICKEN NOODLE SUPERSOUP

This isn't your grandmother's chicken noodle soup; it's spicy, with lots of vegetables including broccoli and leeks. Even though it has a lot of ingredients, it couldn't be simpler to make. Serve it hot and steamy and it will still "cure" the common cold (since it's the steam, not the soup, that makes a stuffy nose feel better).

4 SERVINGS ¢

- 2 **medium leeks (white and light green parts only)**
- 2 **carrots, peeled and thinly sliced**
- ½ **cup thickly sliced celery**
- 4 **cups chicken broth**
- 3 **cups 1-inch chunks cooked boneless chicken**
- 4 **ounces fine or medium egg noodles**
- 2 **cups chopped broccoli florets**
- 1 **teaspoon minced garlic**
- ¼ **teaspoon red pepper flakes**
- ½ **teaspoon dried thyme**
  Salt and freshly ground black pepper

1. Cut the leeks in half lengthwise, wash well, and then slice thinly. Set a large pot over medium heat and add the leeks, carrots, celery, broth, and 2 cups water. Bring to a boil, then reduce the heat to a simmer. Add the chicken, noodles, broccoli, garlic, and red pepper flackes. Cook over low heat until the noodles are tender, 5 to 10 minutes depending upon the type of noodles you use. Stir in the thyme. Remove from the heat and add salt and black pepper to taste.
2. Ladle into bowls to serve.

   + +

TIPS >
Take your leftover vegetables and puree them in a blender with a little chicken broth. Pour them into an ice-cube tray and freeze. Use to thicken a sauce or to add to soup. It's also a great way to make inexpensive baby food!

TORTA RUSTICA

A torte is a cake with a lot of layers. We love this "rustic" version that is actually a layered sandwich "cake." Slice it up and you've got your family lunches for days, or serve it to a dozen people at a party instead of one of those foot-long subs. Feel free to make it with some of your leftovers, too; slice up that roast beef or chicken or whatever else is handy. Just go for a combination of flavors. Whatever meats you use, your total amount should be 1¾ pounds.

I want to say a word about frozen bread dough, too, which is a great thing to have on hand. It's inexpensive and comes in packages of multiple loaves. You can pretty much put it in your freezer and forget it, but then you can pull it out and do all sorts of things with it—make a nice fresh loaf, cut it up into rolls, roll it up with sugar and cinnamon, or, as in this case, wrap it around some filling and make a supersandwich!

12 ¢ SERVINGS

3　10-ounce packages frozen chopped spinach, thawed
2　tablespoons olive oil, plus extra for the dough
1　clove garlic, chopped
½　pound mushrooms, sliced
2　red peppers (bell or spicy, your choice), seeded and chopped
1　large onion, chopped
2　1-pound loaves frozen bread dough, thawed
½　to ¾ pound cooked salami
½　to ¾ pound thinly sliced ham
1　pound sliced mozzarella cheese
½　to ¾ pound thickly sliced turkey breast
1　large egg, beaten with 1 tablespoon water

1. Preheat the oven to 350°F. Lightly grease a 10-inch high-sided springform pan.

2. Squeeze out any extra moisture from the spinach with some paper towels. Put the spinach in a medium-size bowl.

3. Heat the oil in a medium-size skillet over medium heat. Add the garlic and cook, stirring, until it starts to get fragrant, about 1 minute. Add the mushrooms, peppers, and onion and cook, stirring, until they are quite soft, about 2½ minutes. Transfer the contents of the skillet to the bowl with the spinach and stir to combine. Let cool.

4. Cut a 1-inch slice off one of the loaves of dough and set aside. Roll out the 2 loaves of dough into one large circle. (It has to be big enough to cover the bottom and sides of the springform pan and then come back together to cover the top). Drape the dough in the springform pan, covering the bottom and letting it hang out over the sides.

5. Use half the salami to make a layer covering the bottom of the dough in the pan. (Salami is the only layer that we use twice.) Cover it, in order, with layers of the ham, the vegetable mixture, the cheese, the turkey, and finish with the rest of the salami. Bring up the rest of the dough over the top and gather it into some kind of little decorative knot in the middle. If it doesn't reach, this is where that little piece of dough you set aside comes in—roll it out and use to cover the center, pinching it with the other dough to hold it together. If there's too much on top, cut off the extra and discard.

6. Brush the top of the dough with just enough olive oil to cover. Set the pan in the center of the oven. When the dough starts to turn brown, brush the top with the beaten egg. Bake for a total of at least 45 minutes, or until the dough has definitely become bread.

7. Let cool thoroughly. Remove from the pan. Slice into narrow wedges to serve. Only slice what you need; the rest will keep, well wrapped and properly refrigerated, for 4 to 5 days.

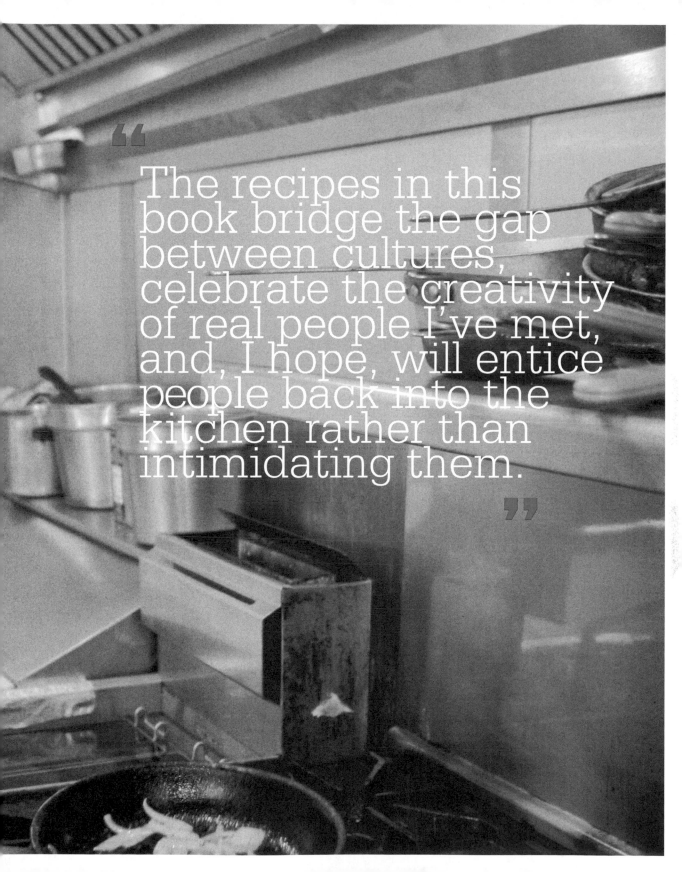

"The recipes in this book bridge the gap between cultures, celebrate the creativity of real people I've met, and, I hope, will entice people back into the kitchen rather than intimidating them."

FRENCH-TOASTED CHICKEN SANDWICHES

We combined the idea of breakfast French toast, when you dip the bread in an egg mixture before you cook it, with the classic French sandwich called *croque monsieur*, in which the bread is slathered with butter and then fried, to come up with this lower-fat tasty sandwich that warms the tummy. We've left it simple, with chicken, tomato, and a little cheese, but you can substitute your favorite cheese or add some cooked peppers, onions, whatever you feel like—just nothing too small that will fall out of the sandwich when you try to turn it over! Garnish with fruit to serve, if you like.

4 SERVINGS ¢

2 **large eggs**
½ **cup milk**
1 **tablespoon freshly grated Parmesan cheese**
⅛ **teaspoon salt**
  Dash of freshly ground black or white pepper
8 **slices sandwich bread**
2 **cups sliced cooked chicken (about ¼ inch thick)**
1 **large tomato, thinly sliced**
2 **sprigs fresh oregano, chopped**
3 **ounces Gruyère, Swiss, or mozzarella cheese (about ¾ cup)**
  Butter

1. In a shallow bowl, mix together the eggs, milk, Parmesan, salt, and pepper. Lay out a baking sheet or piece of aluminum foil large enough to hold 4 slices of bread. Dip one side of each of 4 pieces of bread into the mixture so that the outside is coated but the bread isn't soggy. Lay the bread egg-side down on the prepared surface.
2. Top each slice of bread with an equal amount of chicken. Cover the chicken with slices of tomato. Sprinkle the tomato with the oregano and cover with the Gruyère.
3. Dip one side of each of the remaining 4 bread slices into the egg mixture, adding more milk if necessary, and place a slice egg-side up on top of each sandwich. Trim off any chicken, tomato, or cheese that extends beyond the edges of the bread.
4. Over medium heat, melt enough of the butter in a medium-size skillet to cover the bottom. Carefully add 1 or 2 sandwiches. When the bottom is golden brown and firm, carefully flip over to cook the other side, adding more butter as necessary. Repeat until all the sandwiches are cooked.
5. Slice and serve warm.

STEAK-IN-THE-GRASS SANDWICH

This is one of my favorite sandwiches, and it definitely makes a meal. You can also make it with chunks of juicy cooked chicken. It works with regular sandwich meat, too, but isn't as yummy. We make it with those long rolls that, depending on where you live, are called subs or grinders or heroes, but there's no reason you couldn't make it on a crusty round roll instead. Here we cook the meat from scratch, but you can certainly use leftovers.

4¢ SERVINGS

1   cup Italian dressing
½   pound round steak or stir-fry beef, cut into strips ½ inch thick and 2 to 3 inches long
2   tablespoons olive oil
1   teaspoon minced garlic
2   tablespoons butter
4   crusty sandwich rolls, sliced lengthwise
    Salt and freshly ground black pepper
8   to 12 thick slices mozzarella cheese

1. . Preheat the oven to 300°F.

2. Pour the dressing into a shallow bowl and add the meat. Cover and set aside to marinate, or refrigerate overnight. Before cooking, drain off and discard the marinade.

3. Lightly coat a medium skillet with the oil and set over medium heat. Add the garlic and cook, stirring, until fragrant, about 1 minute. Add the beef and cook, stirring, until it is no longer rare, about 2 minutes. Remove the meat with a slotted spoon or spatula to a plate.

4. Add the butter to the pan and cook over medium heat until it is melted but not brown. Put the bottom halves of the rolls on a baking sheet. Dip a brush into the pan mixture and brush the cut side of all 8 halves of the rolls with the garlicky butter.

5. Divide the meat equally among the 4 rolls. Pour the remaining pan oil, including the garlic, over the meal, and season to taste with salt and pepper.

6. Cover each sandwich with equal amounts of cheese, removing any pieces that extend over the edges. Top with the remaining halves of the rolls. Reduce the oven temperature to "low" or "warm" and bake for 5 to 10 minutes, until the bread is toasty and the cheese is melted. Serve warm.

TARRAGON CHICKEN BAGUETTES

This is a nicely sophisticated sandwich that can be served warm or cold. The chicken can be poached well ahead of time. You can divide one long French baguette into four pieces, but we prefer to buy the individual baguette-type French rolls, or any good crusty roll for that matter. You can also make this chicken salad with leftover chicken.

4 ¢ SERVINGS

1   or 2 cups chicken broth
1   cup dry white wine (optional)
1   pound boneless, skinless chicken breast halves (four 4 ounce halves)
1   tablespoon butter
1   tablespoon all-purpose flour
1   tablespoon Dijon mustard
1   tablespoon chopped fresh tarragon
4   individual-size baguettes or rolls
    Salt and freshly ground black pepper

1. In a deep skillet, bring 2 cups broth (or 1 cup each of broth and white wine) to a boil. Add the chicken, cover the skillet, and reduce the heat to a simmer. Poach the chicken until it is no longer pink inside, 10 to 12 minutes. Transfer the chicken to a plate; pour off the liquid into a separate container and reserve.

2. Add the butter to the empty skillet over medium heat. When the butter has melted, whisk in the flour. Gradually pour the poaching liquid back into the skillet, whisking, until it forms a fairly thick sauce. Stir in the mustard until the mixture is well blended, then stir in the tarragon. Return the chicken to the pan and, if it's not fully immersed in the sauce (which will depend on the size of your skillet), turn it over so that both sides are coated. Reduce the heat to low and cook just long enough to reheat the chicken all the way through.

3. Serve each chicken breast with some of the sauce on a baguette. Season with salt and pepper to taste.

TIPS > + +
Kids love apples with peanut butter. To give it more of a stick-to-your-ribs lunch factor, spread the peanut butter on a sliced bagel and top with apple slices.

TURKEY RAREBIT

This is one of those recipes you come up with when you're trying to figure out new things to do with leftover holiday turkey. You can certainly make it with chicken or just about any sandwich meat. It also works great for appetizers if you cut each piece into quarters!

Rarebit has British origins. While the term is used nowadays to refer to any open-faced sandwich with toast and melted cheese, a real rarebit always has beer and Worcestershire sauce mixed in with the cheese. We've followed those rules, but it works just fine if you substitute an equal amount of milk for the beer.

SERVINGS

5 tablespoons butter, plus extra for the toast

8 slices white bread, lightly toasted

2 or more cups sliced cooked turkey (enough to cover 8 bread slices)

8 thin slices ham (optional)

6 finely chopped scallions (white and light green parts only)

¼ cup all-purpose flour

2 cups milk

1 cup flat beer
Dash of Worcestershire sauce

4 ounces grated cheddar cheese (1 cup)

¼ cup freshly grated Parmesan, Romano, or Asiago cheese
Salt and freshly ground black pepper

1. Preheat the broiler.

2. Butter the toast on both sides and place all 8 slices on a baking sheet. Top each slice of toast with equal amounts of turkey. Top each with a slice of ham, if desired.

3. Melt the 5 tablespoons of butter in a medium-size pot over medium heat. Add the scallions and cook, stirring, until tender but not entirely limp, about 4 minutes. Reduce the heat to low. Gradually add the flour, stirring until it is thoroughly blended, and cook, stirring occasionally, until the flour is cooked and the mixture is golden, about 3 minutes. Slowly add the milk and beer, stirring constantly, and bring to a simmer. Once it begins to thicken, add the Worcestershire sauce, stirring to blend, then gradually stir in ½ cup of the cheddar. Add the Parmesan and keep stirring until the cheeses are melted. Add salt and pepper to taste.

4. Pour the cheese sauce over all 8 open sandwiches. Sprinkle evenly with the remaining ½ cup cheddar. Place the baking sheet 6 inches from the heat source and broil until the cheese is melted but not burned. Serve two per person.

CHEESY TOMATO PANINI

Panini are Italian sandwiches. Literally, the word *panini* is the plural of *panino*, which means "little bread." In Italy you find many types of bread used, but in the United States, it's most popular to make them with focaccia bread, which often has onions, herbs, and other flavors baked into it. Many sandwich shops use panini presses to make a sort of stuffed sandwich, but we handle them the same way we make grilled cheese: just putting a weight on top when cooking. We've also made this from round loaves of Italian bread. You can also use any hard or firm cheese—whatever's handy and appeals to your taste buds! We suggest Havarti, but you could use Jack cheese, Asiago, cheddar, etc.

4 ¢ SERVINGS

8 slices focaccia bread
2 large tomatoes, thinly sliced
12 ounces Havarti cheese
   Olive oil
2 teaspoons chopped fresh basil (optional)

1. Lightly grease a griddle or large skillet with olive oil cooking spray and set over medium heat. Place 4 slices of the bread—or as many as will fit—in the skillet. Cover each of the 4 slices of bread with the sliced tomatoes, and then with equal amounts of cheese. Sprinkle with a little olive oil and, if desired, the basil. Top with the remaining slices of bread.

2. Use whatever is handy to put weight on the top of the sandwiches—a heavy skillet, a bacon press, or a plate with a can or cup of water on top. Cook until the bottoms are golden brown, 3 to 4 minutes. Remove the weight and flip the sandwiches over; cook until the other sides are golden brown.
3. Slice to serve.

AVOCADO-PEAR QUESADILLAS

A little bit of this rich variation on a traditional Mexican snack goes a long way, so it can easily make for a filling dinner alongside a simple soup or salad. Or use a pizza cutter to cut into smaller wedges, and presto—a great, easy hors d'oeuvre. If you can assemble a peanut butter and jelly sandwich, you have all the skills you need to make this recipe!

4 ¢ SERVINGS

8　small flour tortillas
1　ripe avocado, peeled, pitted, and mashed
4　slices bacon, well cooked and crumbled
4　ounces shredded cheddar cheese (1 cup)
2　large very ripe pears, peeled and mashed (if you can't mash them, they're not ripe enough)

1. Preheat the oven to 300°F.
2. Place 4 of the tortillas on a nonstick baking sheet. Spread each with mashed avocado, then sprinkle one-quarter of the crumbled bacon and one-quarter of the shredded cheese evenly over the top of each. Spread each of the remaining tortillas with the mashed pear.

Place, pear-side down, over the tortillas on the pan, as if assembling sandwiches.
3. Bake for 5 to 7 minutes, or until the cheese is melted. Let cool slightly and then slice each "tortilla sandwich" in half. Be careful not to burn your tongue, since the cheese will be very hot.

RATATOUILLE ROLLS

Here's a vegetarian sandwich that's a spin on ratatouille, but the eggplant that's typical of ratatouille is replaced with mushrooms for faster cooking. Strict vegans can omit the cheese; dieters can omit the roll!

4 SERVINGS **¢**

1 28-ounce can plum tomatoes, drained and chopped
1 pound cremini or portobello mushrooms, stems trimmed and cut into bite-size pieces
2 medium zucchini, sliced ⅛ inch thick
½ large onion, thinly sliced
½ teaspoon salt
¼ teaspoon garlic powder
   Freshly ground black pepper
2 tablespoons olive oil
4 large crusty sandwich rolls
8 ounces shredded mozzarella or cheddar cheese (2 cups)

1. Add the tomatoes, mushrooms, zucchini, and onion to a large microwave-safe bowl. Add the salt, garlic powder, and a couple of grinds of pepper. Drizzle with the oil, cover with a vented lid or loosely with some plastic wrap, and microwave on high for 10 minutes.
2. Meanwhile, using a sharp serrated knife, cut off the top inch of each roll and set aside. Use your fingers to remove most of the bread from inside the rest of the roll, leaving about a half-inch thickness on all sides.
3. Sprinkle half the cheese into the bottom of the rolls. Fill each roll not quite to the top with the ratatouille. Top with the remaining cheese and cover with the roll tops you removed earlier.

DAZZLINGLY
Healthy
DESSERTS

"You can eat dessert if you're sensible about it."

Sometimes it just doesn't seem like a meal without dessert. In our "Poor Chef challenge" to create meals for under $7, we don't include dessert in the budget—but

that doesn't mean you can't. As you've seen in previous chapters, a lot of our recipes come in well under budget. Dessert is also something you can save for a splurge.

Having said that, I don't think I need to tell anyone that dessert can be fattening or that too much sugar isn't good for you. Instead, what I want to say is that you can eat dessert if you're sensible about it. Ease up on those sugary baked goods, those pies with lots of butter in the crust, and that high-fat ice cream, and explore what else the world of sweet has to offer. Homemade des-

serts are a lot less expensive than the store-bought variety anyway!

Fruit, of course, is the great good-for-you alternative sweet. Too many people stop right there—fruit for dessert becomes just the piece of fruit, or a bunch of grapes. But when you start thinking of fruit as an ingredient, of ways you can mix it up and chop it up and blend it up and put it in salad, you're on your way to broadening those dessert horizons.

When you just have to have something like cake or pastry, think bread, or think breakfast. Bread

with melted butter and cinnamon is a lot lower in calories than cake, and less expensive, too. Whole wheat waffles with frozen yogurt and a fruit topping—yum. Pancakes spread with grape jelly and rolled up—kids love 'em. Graham crackers are another versatile thing you can turn into an easy dessert once you add some jam or some peanut butter and chocolate.

Just think healthy and fresh and homemade when you think dessert!

BANANA-RAISIN BREAD PUDDING

Yummy, fruity, and filling, this is much lower in sugar and fat than typical desserts. Make it with whole-grain bread to up your fiber content!

SERVINGS

⅔ cup apple juice
¾ cup raisins
2 cups cubed stale bread
1 teaspoon ground cinnamon
1 large ripe banana, mashed
⅔ cup skim milk
1 tablespoon light brown sugar

1. Preheat the oven to 375°F. Lightly grease an 8 x 8-inch square baking dish.

2. Add the apple juice and raisins to a small saucepan over medium-high heat. Bring to a boil, then remove from the heat. Add the bread, cinnamon, and banana and stir until well blended.

3. Pour the mixture into the baking dish. Pour the milk over the top and sprinkle with the brown sugar. Reduce the oven temperature to 350°F and bake for about 45 minutes, until the top is slightly crisp and the interior has a pudding-like consistency. Let rest for at least 10 minutes before serving.

4. Serve warm or cool, by the scoop or cut into squares.

CRUNCHY-FRUIT PARFAITS

These parfaits can be made with any kind of fruit and, if you choose, flavored yogurt. Kids love to eat them—and to make them. They can even be a sneaky way to serve kids a healthy breakfast!

Try all sorts of variations—blueberry yogurt layered with fresh blueberries, strawberry yogurt layered with sliced banana, vanilla yogurt with fresh or canned peaches and peach syrup or honey—the sky's the limit! For adult tastes, I like this version with vanilla yogurt and kiwi, or peach yogurt and mango.

Vary the quantity in your layers depending upon whether you use tall, narrow glasses or short, fat ones; for the latter, you'll want to make larger and fewer layers to get the same visual appeal.

SERVINGS

2 cups low-fat vanilla yogurt
4 hard granola bars, crushed, or 1 cup granola
4 kiwi fruits, peeled and diced

1. Set out four stemmed glasses (wineglasses, champagne flutes, or parfait glasses look best). Spoon about 3 tablespoons yogurt into each glass. Add 1 or 2 tablespoons crushed granola on top of the yogurt, then top each cup with one-quarter of the diced kiwi. Repeat the layers until all the ingredients are used.

TIPS >

Measure your snack portions. This is a really easy way to keep your cravings from taking you beyond your budget—and your belt size. Pick a time when you're not hungry—ideally, right after breakfast, when junk-food cravings are usually at a minimum—and use plastic baggies or aluminum foil to create portions in advance. You can divide them by calories or by money, whichever motivates you more. For example: You have a package of chocolate chip cookies that cost $3.99. It has 34 cookies at 80 calories each. Put 2½ cookies in one baggie for a 200-calorie snack. If you're not counting calories, put 9 cookies in a bag—that's $1 worth. You're less likely to go back for seconds when your internal calculator is adding up the calories, or the cost.

CINNAMON-GLAZED APPLE RINGS

These tasty apple rings make a fairly healthy snack and are a terrific topping for a scoop of yogurt (frozen or otherwise).

4-6 SERVINGS

½   cup apple juice
1   tablespoon lemon juice
¼   teaspoon ground cinnamon
4   tablespoons butter
4   apples, peeled, cored, and
     cut into ½-inch-thick rings
1   tablespoon light brown
     sugar

1. In a small mixing bowl, put the apple juice, lemon juice, and cinnamon and stir to combine.
2. Melt the butter in a large skillet over medium heat. Add the apple rings and cook until golden, about 2 minutes per side. Pour the juice mixture over apples, then sprinkle with the brown sugar. Cover and cook until the apples are tender and glazed, about 5 minutes. Serve warm.

SKIM STRAWBERRY SHERBET

This is an easy, light dessert that could be made with any type of berry. If you're watching your intake of sugar—or calories—you can easily swap the equivalent amount of sweetener for some or all of the sugar. If you freeze some skim milk ahead of time, you'll always be ready to whip this up!

SERVINGS

2 cups skim milk
2 cups sliced fresh strawberries
¼ cup sugar

1. Freeze the skim milk, 1 cup per ice-cube tray.
2. Remove the ice-cube trays from the freezer and let sit at room temperature for just a couple of minutes. Put the cubes into a food processor or blender and pulse until they are the consistency of chunks (do not overblend at this point).

3. Add the berries, ½ cup at a time, pulsing just enough to make room for the next batch of berries. Add the sugar. Blend until smooth. Serve in small bowls or parfait glasses.

TIPS >
This is simple but true—if it's not there, you can't eat it. If you don't BUY junk food, you can't EAT junk food when a craving hits. A key element to this is to shop when you're not hungry. If you know that you and your family like to snack, stock up on fruits and healthy foods. Store-brand ice pops and raisins are two things than can pass for junk but really aren't—and can save the budget, too.

MELON SALAD WITH HONEY-POPPY SEED DRESSING

In some countries, such as France, salads are served after the main course. That's a healthy habit I wish I could get into. Meanwhile, here's a sweet salad that doubles as a healthy dessert. You could also serve this over greens as a light lunch salad.

SERVINGS

1   cup cubes or balls cut from a seeded watermelon
1   cup cubes or balls cut from a honeydew melon
½   cup orange juice
2   tablespoons honey
1   teaspoon poppy seeds
4   fresh mint leaves (optional)

1. In a large mixing bowl, combine the melons, juice, honey, and poppy seeds. Mix well and spoon into four dessert cups or large-bowled wine glasses. Chill. Garnish with a fresh mint leaf on top of each cup, if desired.

> "Sometimes it just doesn't seem like a meal without dessert."

PINEAPPLE UPSIDE-DOWN CUPCAKES

Okay, so these are really more like muffins, but they look like cupcakes, and if kids think they are cupcakes, then this is a good way to wean them off more sugary pastries! These "cupcakes" use buttermilk biscuit mix instead of cake mix.

SERVINGS

4 tablespoons butter
½ cup drained, crushed unsweetened pineapple
¼ cup packed light brown sugar
1 cup Bisquick or other buttermilk baking mix

1. Preheat the oven to 350°F.

2. Put the butter in a small microwave-safe bowl or measuring cup and microwave on high for 30 seconds, cooking for 10 seconds more at a time, if necessary, until the butter is melted.

3. Lightly grease the cups of a 12-hole cupcake tin. Spoon 1 teaspoon of the melted butter into each compartment. Then spoon ½ tablespoon of the pineapple into each, and top each with 1 teaspoon of the brown sugar.

4. In a medium-size bowl, beat the baking mix with ⅓ cup cold water until it forms a smooth batter. Divide the batter equally among the 12 cupcake cups, about 1½ tablespoons each. Bake for 15 to 20 minutes, until a toothpick inserted into the top third of the cupcake comes out clean.

5. Remove from the oven and immediately invert the cupcake tin onto a cookie sheet. Do not remove the cupcake tin immediately; let stand for 5 minutes, then remove the tin. Serve the upside-down cupcakes warm or cool.

STARBURST
FRUIT
SALAD

Sometimes, it's all in the presentation. Food that looks pretty is more appealing. You can also turn a simple dish into something impressive by giving it a visual design. This simple combination of bananas and frozen berries never fails to elicit oohs and ahhs. Garnish with fresh berries, if they're in season!

SERVINGS

1   **10-ounce package frozen raspberries**
2   **large ripe bananas**
3   **teaspoons lemon juice**
1   **tablespoon sliced almonds (optional)**

1. Thaw the berries and drain them well; reserve ¼ cup of the syrup or juice.

2. Peel the bananas. Cut the ends off at a 45-degree angle and, following that angle, cut each banana into long, thin diagonal slices. Arrange the banana slices on a serving platter in a starburst pattern. Brush the exposed sides of the banana slices with 2 teaspoons of the lemon juice to prevent browning.

3. Make a large, rounded scoop out of the well-drained raspberries and place in the center of the "starburst." Mix together the reserved raspberry liquid with the remaining 1 teaspoon lemon juice and spoon over the berries. Sprinkle the bananas, if desired, with the almond slices.

4. Serve immediately or cover and refrigerate for up to 1 hour. Transfer the banana slices to individual plates with a cake server and top each with a spoonful of berries.

BEST BAKED APPLES

SERVINGS

Baked apples are one of those desserts I always forget about, but they are just great and really couldn't be easier. You can bake them up with some lemon juice, cinnamon, and a few raisins in the hole where the core was, or go crazy with nuts, nutmeg, brown sugar or maple syrup, and whipped cream topping. You can make them in the oven, in the microwave, or even in a slow cooker.

Apples are high in fiber, low in fat, and low in calories—what's not to like? A medium-size apple has just 80 calories and as much fiber as a bowl of the typical bran cereal (5 grams); baked with just raisins and cinnamon, they're about 100 calories, and even all dressed up with nuts, sugar, and a dollop of whipped cream, they come in at just over 200 calories. Apples even contain an essential trace element, boron, that helps to harden our bones, making them great for growing children and for helping to fight osteoporosis as we get older.

4   **medium apples**
¼   **cup plus 4 teaspoons lemon juice (from about 3 lemons)**
¼   **cup raisins**
1   **teaspoon ground cinnamon**
¼   **cup chopped walnuts (optional)**
4   **teaspoons light or dark brown sugar or maple syrup (optional)**
½   **teaspoon ground nutmeg (optional)**
    Whipped cream, for serving (optional)

1. . Preheat the oven to 350°F.

2. Cut off the top quarter of each apple. (Save the tops for snacks or to chop up for a salad.) Use an apple corer or melon baller to remove the core, being careful not to cut all the way through the bottom. For visual effect, if you like, use a vegetable peeler to remove a strip of peel from around the top. (Rub 1 teaspoon of the lemon juice on the tops and insides of each apple to prevent browning.) Put the apples either in individual ovenproof custard cups or tightly packed together in a small baking dish.

3. Pour ½ cup water per apple and 1 tablespoon lemon juice per apple into the custard cups or baking dish. In a small bowl, mix together the raisins and cinnamon and add, if you like, the nuts, brown sugar, and/or nutmeg (use maple syrup instead of brown sugar for cooking in the microwave; see instructions below). Divide the filling equally among the apples, filling up the holes.

4. Bake, basting occasionally with the pan liquid, for about 1 hour or until the apples are spoon-tender but not collapsing. Serve warm, topped, if desired, with a little whipped cream.

Notes: To cook in the microwave: Substitute apple juice or apple cider for the water and cook on high for 10 minutes or until the apples are tender.

To cook in the slow cooker: Reduce the amount of water to 2 tablespoons. Put ½ teaspoon butter on top of the filling of each apple. Cover and cook on low for 8 hours.

GRAHAM CRACKER FRUIT TORTE

I love making desserts with graham crackers (which were invented by a man named Graham). Since they're usually made from whole wheat, they're so much better for you than a cookie, and they're versatile, too. You can break graham crackers into halves along their perforations, cover one half with peanut butter, and pour some melted chocolate over it to make a fancy cookie, if you are so inclined. I even have a friend who went crazy one year and made a whole "gingerbread house" village out of graham crackers.

This recipe is for a torte, which is, strictly speaking, a layered cake, but using graham crackers lets you make an easy no-bake cake in a flash. In between the layers you can use jelly, jam, or preserves; it's plenty sweet with the no-sugar-added preserves. You can alternate fruit flavors or just stick with a favorite.

Kids love helping to assemble this because it's sort of like making a tower. Most graham crackers come in rectangles with two perforated squares attached to each other; use the whole rectangles intact to make this torte.

SERVINGS

⅔ cup fresh raspberries or blueberries, plus more for garnish (optional)

4 ounces ready-made refrigerated whipped topping

12 double graham crackers (about 5 x 2½ inches) No-sugar-added strawberry or other fruit preserves

1. Put the berries in a blender and puree. Put the whipped topping into a medium-size bowl. Gradually stir the berry puree into the topping. Refrigerate, covered, until ready to use.

2. Lay out 11 of the graham crackers. Spread 6 crackers with a thick layer of preserves (about 2 tablespoons each). Spread 5 crackers with a thick layer of the berry–whipped cream topping (about 2 tablespoons each).

3. Start assembling the torte. Put one of the crackers that is covered with preserves on a serving plate. Top it with one of the topping-covered crackers. Continue to alternate, finishing with a preserve-covered cracker. Top with the twelfth cracker. Using one or two large spatulas, carefully turn the tower onto its side. With a flat knife, spread the remaining berry topping over all the exposed sides. Refrigerate for at least 8 hours, and preferably overnight.

4. Slice with a sharp knife to serve. Garnish, if you like, with fresh berries.

CINNAMON-RAISIN MONKEY-BREAD

SERVINGS 6-8

Monkeybread is great stuff that looks and sounds a whole lot more complicated than it really is. Monkeybread gets its name because you pull it apart into balls that you pop into your mouth, sort of like the way a monkey eats fruit.

Making monkeybread is fun, too, and something that you can really get the kids into for some quality family time in the kitchen. You roll dough into balls or cut it into any kind of shapes, flavor them, and then just pile them up in a pan. You really can't do it wrong, which makes it a rewarding project for youngsters.

You can certainly use homemade bread dough to make monkeybread, but we recommend using frozen bread dough or, even easier, refrigerator biscuits.

By the way, monkeybread doesn't have to be sweet; you can also make it with garlic butter and Parmesan, for example, to go with dinner.

1   **1-pound loaf frozen bread dough, or four 11.5-ounce cans refrigerator biscuits**
8   **tablespoons (1 stick) butter, melted**
1   **cup granulated sugar**
¾   **cup packed light or dark brown sugar**
2   **teaspoons ground cinnamon**
1   **cup raisins**
½   **cup chopped walnuts**

1. Preheat the oven to 350°F. Lightly grease a tube pan, Bundt pan, or deep round cake pan.
2. Cut the bread dough into 1-inch pieces, or cut the biscuits into halves or quarters, and roll each piece into a ball.
3. Add the melted butter to a small bowl. In another bowl, mix together the sugars and the cinnamon. Dip each ball of dough first into the melted butter and then into the flavored sugar. Reserve the leftover sugar. Make one layer of dough balls, touching each other, on the bottom of the pan.
4. How many layers you'll make will depend on the size of the dough balls you made; you'll probably be making either 3 or 4 layers. Mix together the raisins and nuts and divide into either 2 (for 3 layers) or 3 (for 4 layers) portions. Sprinkle a portion over the first layer. Repeat with another layer of dough balls and another layer of raisins and nuts, finishing with a top layer of dough balls. Sprinkle the remaining sugar mixture over the top.
5. Bake for 30 minutes or until individual pieces are no longer doughy inside. (Stick a knife or skewer into the middle; if it comes out clean, it's done.) Let it rest briefly, then turn it out of the pan to a plate; serve warm or cool.

INDEX